Preservation: The Kinks' Music 1964-1974

Andrew Hickey

Copyright © Andrew Hickey 2012, all rights reserved.
The author has asserted his moral rights.

All song lyrics are copyright their respective owners, and are quoted for review purposes in accordance with fair dealing and fair use laws. No claim over them is asserted.

Note for the 2018 edition: This text is identical to the original 2012 edition, with a single exception: the original edition unwittingly used a transphobic term in the entry for the song "Lola". I have replaced three words to remove the transphobia and deleted one explanatory footnote I now believe to be unnecessary. Otherwise the text remains unchanged.

BY THE SAME AUTHOR:
Sci-Ence! Justice Leak!
The Beatles In Mono
An Incomprehensible Condition: An Unauthorised Guide To Grant Morrison's Seven Soldiers
The Beach Boys On CD Vol 1: The 1960s
Monkee Music
Doctor Watson Investigates: The Case Of The Scarlet Neckerchief (ebook only)
Classic Albums: Pet Sounds (ebook only)
Ideas And Entities: A Collection Of Short Stories

For Holly

Contents

Introduction 7

Beat Group (1964-65) 9

Kinks 11

Kinda Kinks 27

The Kink Kontroversy 43

The Classic Pye Albums (1966 - 1970) 57

Face To Face 59

Something Else 73

Village Green Preservation Society 89

Arthur 113

Lola Vs Powerman 131

Percy 147

The Early RCA Albums (1971-74)   155

Muswell Hillbillies   157

Everybody's In Showbiz   171

Preservation   181

Appendix: Non-Album Songs   211

Acknowledgements   215

Introduction

It's become a cliché to say that the Kinks are the most underrated of the great 1960s beat groups, but that cliché has some truth to it. While the music the Kinks made during their artistic peak, from roughly 1966 through 1970, has become accepted as essential listening by most critics, there is no real body of criticism looking at the evolution of the band's sound.

While one could quite easily build up a substantial library of books analysing the work of peers like the Beatles, Rolling Stones, the Who or Bob Dylan, there are no real works of criticism dealing with the music of the Kinks. This book is an attempt to make a start towards rectifying that — a start that with luck others will build on.

This is a critical analysis of every song the band recorded in the studio between 1964 and 1974 which has had a legal release (so live recordings, bootlegs and so on aren't covered — unless they have been released as tracks on studio albums.) In each case, I am using the most recent CD issues (for the Pye albums, the deluxe multi-CD editions with both mono and stereo mixes and a large number of bonus tracks.) For all the 1960s recordings except *Arthur* I am taking the mono versions as the definitive ones — most records in the 60s were mixed with mono in mind, and certainly the mono mixes sound better — but there is usually little difference, and I have noted when any major differences have jumped out after listening to both mixes of a given track.

This book doesn't pretend to objectivity – I will say frankly where I dislike a song, even when that is a favourite of many, and likewise I will make it clear when I think a song is underrated or unfairly overlooked.

It is also not meant to be a comprehensive reference to the band's career. This is not a listing of session dates or musicians who played on particular tracks. That information is included if it's relevant, but thorough guides to those things are available elsewhere, and I have not attempted to duplicate them here.

What this is intended to be is a song-by-song look at the band's work during their most productive and artistically successful decade, looking at where it succeeds and where it fails, and trying to analyse how. I hope that it will help people listen to the Kinks' music with new ears, and find new subtleties in it, as writing the book has for me.

Beat Group (1964-65)

Kinks

The Kinks' first album, titled simply *Kinks*, is a mish-mash of different styles, only some of them effective. While Ray and Dave Davies had been playing together for many years, and had been working with bass player Pete Quaife for some time, the final line-up of the band, with drummer Mick Avory, had only settled down after the release of the band's debut single, a lacklustre cover of *Long Tall Sally*, in February 1964. Avory was so new to the band that he doesn't even appear on much of the album, being replaced by session player Bobbie Graham.

The band's early singles set the pattern for this album. *Long Tall Sally* was a semi-competent cover of an American R&B classic, *You Still Want Me,* the band's second single, was decent Merseybeat-by-numbers, and *You Really Got Me*, their third, was one of the greatest singles of all time, a crunchy garage-rock track with one of the best riffs ever committed to record.

And the album is as much of a mixed bag as the singles. Like many British bands in 1964 and '65, the Kinks were attempting to sound like the American blues music of a previous generation. The problem is that like many of those bands, the Kinks were not particularly strong either vocally or instrumentally, and simply couldn't carry the weight of this material. When Muddy Waters or Bo Diddley sing "I'm A Man", the implicit meaning is "so don't call me 'boy'". When white teenagers from the Home Counties sing the same material, it comes out sounding more like "I'm a grown man, now, mummy, so you can't make me tidy my room!"

The best of the British R&B-oriented bands, like the Animals or the Zombies or the Spencer Davis Group, got away with this by having astonishingly good vocalists - and all of these bands soon moved away from the R&B sound. The Kinks, too, would make this move very soon, but in 1964 there was little to impress on their first album.

And while they don't add very much to the sound, it should probably be mentioned that among the session players who played on this album are Jimmy Page (who added acoustic rhythm guitar on a couple of tracks but did not play any leads, despite some reports to the contrary) and Jon Lord.

The Album

Beautiful Delilah

Writer: Chuck Berry

Lead Vocalist: Dave Davies

The album opener is a perfect example of where most British blues bands of the time were going wrong. A cover version of one of Chuck Berry's more minor works, this misses everything that makes Berry's original worth listening to - the wit in Berry's vocals, and his distinctive guitar work.

It does have a punk energy, especially in Dave Davies' incoherent vocals, but even so it sounds forced. This is garage band music in a bad way - it's the work of teenagers who aren't very good yet, and who love R&B music without knowing what it is they love about it.

So Mystifying

Writer: Ray Davies

Lead Vocalist: Ray Davies

This is a much better attempt at the same kind of thing. It appears to have been written off the Rolling Stones' version of *It's All Over Now*, but has a more country-blues flavour, reminiscent both of early Chuck Berry tracks like *Maybelline* and of Carl Perkins rockabilly. The lead guitar part, in particular, has some unusual choices that point the way forward to the band's later experimentation with country music on albums like *Muswell Hillbillies*.

The song, and the track, are still not especially good, but even on a by-the-numbers blues track like this Ray Davies is starting to develop a distinctive voice which suits the band far better than the cover versions they do.

Just Can't Go To Sleep

Writer: Ray Davies

Lead Vocalist: Ray Davies

A simple exercise in a girl-group style, this is the kind of thing that bands like the Swinging Blue Jeans were having hits with at the time, and is a very competent piece in the style, but completely unmemorable except for the key change down a tone for the middle section, which is an unusually-long twelve bars. The hook line sounds like an early attempt at the hook for *Stop Your Sobbing*.

Long Tall Shorty

Writers: Don Covay and Herbert C Abramson

Lead Vocalist: Dave Davies

This song was originally recorded by Tommy Tucker earlier in 1964 as a follow-up to his hit single *Hi-Heeled Sneakers*, and has almost exactly the same melody as that track. Probably the best of the R&B covers on this album, this has some very creditable harmonica playing from Ray Davies – nothing technically challenging, but with far more feeling than much of the music elsewhere on the album. It's still fundamentally pointless though, especially in comparison with Tucker's much more interesting original.

I Took My Baby Home

Writer: Ray Davies

Lead Vocalist: Ray Davies

Easily the catchiest and most commercial sounding of the tracks so far, this is a simple three-chord formula pop song of a kind that almost every band did dozens of during the sixties (probably its closest relation is *I'm A Fool* by Dino, Desi and Billy from a couple of years later, but every Merseybeat band had a few songs like this.) The arrangement is more inventive than normal for this kind of song, though, with all instruments except the drums dropping out for the "I wo-o-o-o-on't" line, and some quite complicated drum fills.

This was the B-side to the band's first single, *Long Tall Sally*, and should really have been the A-side, being both a better performance and more in tune with the music that was having success in early 1964.

I'm A Lover Not A Fighter

Writer: Jay Miller

Lead Vocalist: Dave Davies

A cover of a Cajun blues song by evil racist scumbag J.D. Miller, this features some very nice guitar picking from Dave Davies, but is unfortunately spoiled by his lead vocal, which has all the subtlety of a rutting rhinoceros.

You Really Got Me

Writer: Ray Davies

Lead Vocalist: Ray Davies

It's almost impossible to describe how much this track stands out from the dross around it. On paper, this should be more of the same - a simple two-note riff, played in three different keys, and a lyric with a 35-word vocabulary (significantly simpler than the average Doctor Seuss book.) In fact the lyric originally only had thirty-four words in it, but Davies was persuaded to change some of the "yeah"s to "girl", to avoid any possible implication of homosexuality.

The sound of this, though, is extraordinary. Forty-eight years later, this still packs a punch unlike anything else in the charts at that time. At a time when record companies were turning down tracks on the grounds that the guitar was distorted, this is recorded with a guitar put through a speaker cone that had been slashed with a knife. Everything about this track is designed to evoke adolescent sexual tension in the extreme - the riff, the repetitive single-note piano parts, Dave Davies' long "yeaaaaaaaaaaaaaaaaaaaaaaaaaah" backing vocals, Ray Davies' screaming, lustful vocals on the high notes. And nothing like Dave Davies' finger-twisting guitar solo had ever been recorded before.

Angry, frustrated, raunchy, this is the precise moment when rock - as opposed to rock 'n' roll - was invented.

Cadillac

Writer: Bo Diddley

Lead Vocalist: Ray Davies

And we're immediately back into the realms of R & B covers, although Bo Diddley's thuggish simplicity is more suited to the band at this stage of their development than many of the other covers have been, and this isn't too bad at all.

Bald Headed Woman

Writer: Shel Talmy

Lead Vocalist: Ray Davies

One of two covers of tracks by the folk singer Odetta, included on the album so that producer Shel Talmy could claim a 'trad. arr.' writing credit. The band do as competent a job as could be expected for a song so firmly out of their normal stylistic range (it sounds more like a work chant than anything else), but this is pointless.

Revenge

Writer: Ray Davies and Larry Page

Lead Vocalist: Instrumental

As is this, a by-the-numbers harmonica-led instrumental presumably included so that Larry Page, one of the band's managers, could get some songwriting money too. It's actually quite an advanced-sounding track - it could easily be a backing track from Love's first album, two years later, but it sounds like a backing track for which someone's forgotten to bother to record a vocal, rather than a proper instrumental.

Too Much Monkey Business

Writer: Chuck Berry

Lead Vocalist: Ray Davies

Another missing-the-point Chuck Berry cover, again of a song which depends almost entirely on Berry's delivery for its effect, this one is even less successful than *Beautiful Delilah* because of the frankly incomprehensible decision to double track the lead vocal. For a wordy song such as this, so dependent on diction, this is fatal. Dave Davies' guitar solo is quite nice though.

I've Been Driving On Bald Mountain

Writer: Odetta Felious

Lead Vocalist: Dave Davies

The second of the Odetta covers, though on this one Odetta has regained her songwriting credit as the song isn't actually traditional. The backing track is quite pleasant, in an acoustic hootenany kind of way, but then Dave Davies does his usual tuneless punk hollering over the top. He got much better as a vocalist.

Stop Your Sobbing

Writer: Ray Davies

Lead Vocalist: Ray Davies

This is the second really good track on the album, and one of Ray Davies' very best early songs. A simple Merseybeat track, this has a gorgeous melody and one of the catchiest hooks Davies ever came up with ("better stop sobbing now".)

It's also more emotionally ambiguous than the rest of his early songs, paving the way for the more interesting work he'd be doing later on. The protagonist wants to help his girlfriend get over whatever is causing her to cry, but he's also implicitly threatening to leave her if she doesn't. There's a weird unresolved tension here between the sympathetic and the extraordinarily callous, that makes this the most emotionally realistic song on the entire album.

This track is also the first to feature Rasa Didzpetris on backing vocals. Didzpetris was soon to become Ray Davies' first wife, and as Rasa Davies her vocal lines became an essential part of many of the Kinks' most memorable records.

While this was never released as a single, the Pretenders released a version in 1979 that was a minor hit.

Got Love If You Want It

Writer: James H Moore

Lead Vocalist: Ray Davies

And we end with another cover version of a blues standard. This one is better than the album standard, because Ray Davies plays with his vocals here in a way he hasn't on the rest of the album, and wins over on sheer strangeness. There's some ferociously good drumming on this track too.

Bonus Tracks

I Believed You

Writer: Ray and Dave Davies

Lead Vocalist: Ray Davies

An early demo recording, before the band had settled on the name the Kinks, this was recorded under the name the Bo Weevils. A much more sophisticated song and performance than most of what we can hear on the actual album, this could easily have been a hit for a band like the Zombies. It suggests that many of the problems with the first album can be laid at the door not of the band themselves, but of producer Shel Talmy, with whom the band didn't get on, and who notably didn't produce *You Really Got Me,* although he was credited with it.

I'm A Hog For You Baby

Writer: Jerry Leiber and Mike Stoller

Lead Vocalist: Ray Davies

Another Bo Weevils demo, this one is a fairly poor-quality recording of a Coasters cover, but it still shows the band as far more assured than on the *Kinks* album, with some very good lead guitar and with the band members doing a variety of silly voices in the style of the original. Where most of the R&B covers on the album show an utter lack of comprehension, this one is a sympathetic cover of what is, ultimately, a fluffy piece of nothing.

I Don't Need You Any More

Writer: Ray Davies

Lead Vocalist: Ray Davies

A demo from January 1964, in very rough quality, this is a decent enough pop-rocker that would have made a perfectly acceptable album track had it been taken any further.

Everybody's Gonna Be Happy (demo)

Writer: Ray Davies

Lead Vocalist: Ray Davies

This is a demo, recorded toward the end of 1964, for what would become the band's sixth single. I'll deal with the song more when I look at the *Kinda Kinks* album, but what I can say is that this demo shows every element of the finished record was conceived very early on - the arrangement barely changed at all, although the performance on the finished track is much tighter.

Long Tall Sally

Writer: Richard Penniman, Robert Blackwell and Enotis Johnson

Lead Vocalist: Ray Davies

For the band's first single, they were persuaded to record *Long Tall Sally*, a Little Richard song that they'd never performed before, on the grounds that the Beatles were performing the song live (this was before the Beatles released their own studio version of the song.)

On paper, an R&B song about a transsexual prostitute should have been perfect for the Kinks, but there's no evidence they'd actually figured out what the lyrics were. While Paul McCartney got round the problem of not being able to understand Little Richard's screeched vocals by gabbling, Ray Davies seems to have just made up some new lyrics for himself.

The song's taken at too slow a pace - in fact the band are playing the riff from a different, slower, Little Richard song, *Lucille*, and for all their singing "we're having some fun tonight" it sounds like they're protesting too much. It's not a bad track, as such, but nor is it a very good one, and it's easy to see why this was a flop, only reaching number 42 despite a TV appearance on *Ready, Steady, Go*.

You Still Want Me

Writer: Ray Davies

Lead Vocalist: Ray Davies

The band's second single, this was even less commercially successful than *Long Tall Sally*, but it's harder to see why in retrospect. This would have been a great pop hit in 1963, the year of Gerry And The Pacemakers, the Swinging Blue Jeans and the Searchers. Unfortunately for the band, it was released in 1964, at a time when a harder, bluesier style was starting to come into fashion, and sounded like they were trying to jump on the bandwagon just after it had pulled away.

With five decades' hindsight, though, this was a massive improvement on their first single, and shows that they were headed in the right direction. While this didn't chart, the lowest chart ranking any of their next thirteen singles would have would be number eleven.

You Do Something To Me

Writer: Ray Davies

Lead Vocalist: Ray Davies

The B-side to *You Still Want Me*, this uptempo pop track is equal parts Merseybeat (in the verses) and Buddy Holly (in the middle eight), with some quite gorgeous Everly Brothers style harmonies from the Davies brothers, in a style they never really returned to. This is easily as good as, say, any of the hits the Hollies had around this time, and is in much the same style.

Quite why this and its A-side were left off the album is hard to say.

It's Alright

Writer: Ray Davies

Lead Vocalist: Ray Davies

The B-side of *You Really Got Me* is a standard Brit-blues riff-based track, possibly showing a little of the influence of Mose Allison, either directly or through contemporary bands like Manfred Mann. There's no real song there - it sounds like something that evolved out of a jam session - but the performance and arrangement, with a prominent drum part and short spot of dead air when the entire band briefly drop out, are inventive enough that the track remains listenable.

All Day And All Of The Night

Writer: Ray Davies

Lead Vocalist: Ray Davies

The follow-up to *You Really Got Me* was very much a repeat of that single's winning formula. Instead of a two-note riff, this time we have a three-note riff (F, G and B♭.) And whereas *You Really Got Me* goes up by a tone, then by another tone, this track goes up by a third, and then up by a tone into the chorus.

Otherwise, this sticks as closely as possible to the *You Really Got Me* template, and amazingly manages to capture lighting in a bottle twice. The band would very soon move on to more complex songs, but like their previous single this is one of the great pop-rock tracks of all time.

I Gotta Move

Writer: Ray Davies

Lead Vocalist: Ray Davies

The B-side to *All Day And All Of The Night* is again very similar to the previous B-side, a simple riffy blues track. By this point, the Kinks had become quite good at this kind of track, but there's little of interest here other than the faint backing vocals, setting up a drone - a sound which would become of more interest to the band in the next year.

Louie Louie

Writer: Richard Berry

Lead Vocalist: Ray Davies

Apparently Ray Davies wrote *You Really Got Me* while trying to work out the three-chord riff to *Louie Louie,* which had been a hit for the Kingsmen in the US the previous year, so it was natural that the Kinks would record their own version, which became the opening track of their *Kinksize Session* EP. This version is now the best-known version in the UK, and is notable for the band getting the chords wrong (they play I-IV-V rather than I-IV-v.) This recording in turn seems to have been the inspiration for the Troggs' hit version of *Wild Thing* in 1966 - a record produced by the Kinks' manager Larry Page.

I've Got That Feeling

Writer: Ray Davies

Lead Vocalist: Ray Davies

The second track on *Kinksize Session*, this seems to be an attempt by Ray Davies to write in the style of the Zombies, who had recently had their first big hit with *She's Not There*. Much like that song, this is keyboard based, and based around a jazzy riff centred on an Am chord, though this continues the habit Davies has at this time of making riffs out of single-tone differences, rather than having the more expansive changes of the Zombies song. This is again reminiscent of the riffs to *You Really Got Me* and *All Day And All Of The Night*, but the choice is probably made because unlike the Zombies' singer Colin Blunstone, Ray Davies was at this time an incredibly limited vocalist, and keeping within a narrow range was probably necessary.

I Gotta Go Now

Writer: Ray Davies

Lead Vocalist: Ray Davies

At 2:53, the third track on *Kinksize Session* is longer than anything on the band's first album. Which is odd, because it must have taken much less time than that to write, consisting as it does mostly of two chords and six words. And unlike in the case of *You Really Got Me,* this doesn't appear to be a deliberate choice as much as it's an utter lack of effort. I actually managed to forget this track while listening to it.

Things Are Getting Better

Writer: Ray Davies

Lead Vocalist: Ray Davies

This track, the last on *Kinksize Session* is actually a rewrite of *Cadillac.* Ray Davies forgets the lyric to the last line on the last verse, and what little lyric there is is written in an attempt at

American dialect (our protagonist "hasn't got a dime".) Davies would soon move away from this kind of imitation and find a voice of his own though.

Don't Ever Let Me Go

Writer: Ray Davies

Lead Vocalist: Ray Davies

This was apparently an attempt at a follow-up to *You Really Got Me*, wisely scrapped in favour of *All Day And All Of The Night*. It features the same riff as *You Really Got Me*, but married to a more conventional, and thus less interesting, song.

I Don't Need You Any More

Writer: Ray Davies

Lead Vocalist: Ray Davies

An utterly by-the-numbers garage rock track, with absolutely nothing of any interest about it.

Little Queenie

Writer: Chuck Berry

Lead Vocalist: Ray Davies

Recorded during a live BBC session, and introduced by Brian Matthew (who is still to this day a BBC DJ, having been a broadcaster for 64 years), this is yet another attempt at a Chuck Berry cover. This time, they miss out half of the lyrics and don't seem to really have understood the rest. The liner notes for the *Kinks* deluxe edition claim Ray Davies is singing this, but if so he sounds *very* like his brother Dave (although the two could often sound alike.)

Overall, *Kinks*, and the material recorded around that time, is a sloppy mess for the most part, with occasional flashes of brilliance, though sloppiness was the norm for every band other than the Beatles or the Beach Boys at the end of 1964. 1965 would see the Kinks improve dramatically. . .

Kinda Kinks

While *Kinda Kinks*, the Kinks' second album, is Ray Davies' least favourite, and it shows clearly the signs of having been written and recorded in a hurry, with some sloppy double-tracking and less-than-stellar compositions, it is a clear step forward in ambition from the first album.

While *Kinks* had been pretty much a bog-standard Brit-blues album with few or no distinguishing features other than its one incredible single, *Kinda Kinks* draws from a much broader range of musical styles. In particular, we see the influences of the new folk finger-picking guitarists who were starting to become known on the London scene, people like Bert Jansch, John Renbourn and Davy Graham. Within a year, these influences would become widespread in pop music, thanks to Donovan and Simon & Garfunkel, but *Kinda Kinks* is the first example I know of of this style in mainstream pop-rock.

On the other hand, we see an increasing influence from Motown here, especially Martha And The Vandellas, whose *Dancing In The Streets* is one of only two covers on this album. (Oddly, the other cover, *Naggin' Woman*, is co-written by evil racist scumbag J.D. Miller, composer of *I'm A Lover Not A Fighter* from the previous album, under a pseudonym.)

But the shocking thing about Ray Davies' songwriting at this time is just how much good material he was producing. While the album itself is patchy, there are some wonderful songs, included as demos on the deluxe edition, which were given to other performers, including some of Davies' best work. Adding in the non-album singles and EP tracks included here leads to this being the first really essential collection by the Kinks, and the first real sign that they would soon become one of the greatest bands of all time.

The Album

Look For Me Baby

Writer: Ray Davies

Lead Vocalist: Ray Davies

The album opener is an unprepossessing track based on a two-chord I-V riff, with a melody owing a little to *Watermelon Man* and girl-group backing vocals. At times Davies rushes to get all his lyrics into the space he has, and the double-tracking is incredibly sloppy, but this is still more competent than most of what was on *Kinks*.

Got My Feet Off The Ground

Writer: Ray and Dave Davies

Lead Vocalist: Dave Davies

A fun little country blues track, this is spoiled by Dave Davies' lead vocals. Over the years he would become a fine, sensitive vocalist in his own right, but at this point he was just yelling. There's some nice Chet Atkins-isms on the guitar solo though.

Nothin' In The World Can Stop Me Worryin' 'Bout That Girl

Writer: Ray Davies

Lead Vocalist: Ray Davies

Another blues-based song, this one uses a pentatonic riff reminiscent of much of Bert Jansch's work of the time, one that works in cross-rhythm to the rest of the track (and in the intro seems to be completely metrically irregular - every time I try to break down the track into bars, before the entrance of the bass and drums, I get a different number.) This is in many ways the most forward-looking of all the tracks on this album - songs sounding exactly like this would make up the bulk of *Led Zeppelin III* many years later.

A lovely, haunting, if rather slight song, this is easily the most interesting and mature thing the band had released to this point.

Naggin' Woman

Writer: Jimmy Anderson & Jerry West

Lead Vocalist: Dave Davies

A cover of a blues classic, *Naggin'*, by bluesman Jimmy Anderson (oddly co-written by Anderson, a black man, and J.D. Miller, a supporter of the Ku Klux Klan, under a pseudonym), this has some fine blues playing - the best that the Kinks ever did in the genre - but is let down by a poor lead vocal from Dave Davies and a less-than-wonderful lyric.

I Wonder Where My Baby Is Tonight

Writer: Ray Davies

Lead Vocalist: Dave Davies

This track is a simple rewrite - one might almost say a cover version - of *Can I Get A Witness* by Marvin Gaye, whose simple piano riff had already become the basis of such tracks as *The Boy From New York City* by the Ad-Libs and *Carl's Big Chance* by the Beach Boys. OK on its own, this doesn't even begin to approach the quality of its inspiration.

Tired Of Waiting For You

Writer: Ray Davies

Lead Vocalist: Ray Davies

According to Davies' autobiography, *X-Ray*, this was actually written before *All Day And All Of The Night* and held back so that the more formulaic track could go first. In truth, while this seemed like a huge departure from the band's formula, it's based around a very similar two-chord riff to *You Really Got Me*, just slowed down, in the verses, with the bridge and middle eight being almost as simplistic.

However, melodically and lyrically this introduced a new element into the Kinks' singles, one that was definitely not present on the earlier hits - there's a yearning, wistful quality to this that would become a hallmark of Davies' writing over the next few years. Supposedly about Davies' longing for success to finally come (though quite how long he could have been waiting, given that *You Really Got Me* was released only a couple of months after his twentieth birthday, is debatable), there's a deeper longing and melancholy in here, one that would become more pronounced as Davies' songwriting progressed.

This, however, is the perfect point between the band's early garage-rock and its later sophistication, and unsurprisingly became a number one hit in the UK, and the band's biggest ever hit in the US at number six.

Dancing In The Street

Writer: Marvin Gaye, Ivy Jo Hunter and Mickey Stevenson

THE ALBUM

Lead Vocalist: Ray Davies

This, on the other hand, is just a horrible mess. A cover of Martha And The Vandellas' hit of the previous year, this might have worked had any of the Kinks had a funky bone in their body, but their idea of dance music was primal aggression rather than soul, and they don't even make a half-hearted attempt to copy the original's distinctive riff or backing vocals.

To make matters worse, Ray Davies apparently seems not to have a clue what the melody is, and to be reading the lyrics off a sheet of paper with little thought as to their scansion. This is then double-tracked, so we have two mumbling Davieses, each unsure of what exactly they're meant to be doing. Pitiful.

Don't Ever Change

Writer: Ray Davies

Lead Vocalist: Ray Davies

One of the more musically interesting songs on the album, this has a somewhat amorphous structure, showing Davies experimenting with the type of non-traditional songwriting that would later lead to such masterpieces as *Autumn Almanac*. It's also far more harmonically interesting than the band's previous work - still keeping the same basic I-V type relationships that many of the band's songs are built on (though introducing an element of harmonic ambiguity with the F chords that let us wonder if this is in G, as it originally appears, or C as is later implied), but using extended chords like sixths, ninths and thirteenths.

It doesn't quite work - it's pleasant enough, but it sounds awkward rather than sophisticated - but it's an intriguing experiment and a sign of Davies' restlessness with the formula he had only recently hit upon.

Come On Now

Writer: Ray Davies

Lead Vocalist: Dave Davies

A simple three-chord garage-rocker, this is one of the catchier of the album tracks here, and is perfectly suited to Dave Davies' raw, yelling voice. It has a catchy riff and good backing vocals, and is very danceable, but has few enough distinguishing features that it's hard to discuss it at any great length.

So Long

Writer: Ray Davies

Lead Vocalist: Ray Davies

A rather lovely attempt at the folk fingerpicking style, this features a guitar part very similar to the instrumental line in Simon & Garfunkel's later *Leaves That Are Green* (compare Paul Simon's solo recording on *The Paul Simon Songbook*, recorded three months after this album's release), and a very unusual structure.

   It starts with a simple eight-bar three-chord chorus, much like many of the band's other songs of the period, but then goes into a twenty-one-bar verse, which hovers between the keys of C and G, never quite resolving into either.

   This folky style was a bit of a dead end for the Kinks, and was largely abandoned after this album, but the acoustic wistfulness of songs like this definitely informed much of the band's later work.

You Shouldn't Be Sad

Writer: Ray Davies

Lead Vocalist: Ray Davies

An attempt at writing a Martha And The Vandellas style girl-group song, this track would be pleasant enough were it not for the truly horrible double-tracking of Ray Davies' lead vocal. I keep going on about this on these early albums, but that's because Shel Talmy's decisions are often utterly incomprehensible. Double-tracking can help with a vocal when there's a problem with pitch or timbre - neither of which are particular problems for Ray Davies, even this early on. On the other hand, he does have problems with his phrasing, often sounding hesitant and not coming in quite on the beat. Double-tracking a vocal like that is a recipe for disaster, and turns tracks like this, which would be perfectly reasonable pop records, into sloppy messes that are actively painful to listen to.

Something Better Beginning

Writer: Ray Davies

Lead Vocalist: Ray Davies

And the album proper ends with another exercise in stylistic pastiche, this time a strong attempt at a Phil Spector sound, combining elements of Spector's Ronettes work (the *Be My Baby* rhythm) with the vaguely Latin feel of Spector's earlier work with Leiber and Stoller (notably *Spanish Harlem*.)

The band do remarkably well, given that they're attempting to ape Spector's style with only a standard rock-band lineup, and while Davies' vocal is double-tracked in places, it's done with a much lighter touch than on other tracks.

This is a solid, enjoyable closer to an album which, while far from perfect, is a giant step forward compared to the band's earlier work.

Bonus Tracks

Everybody's Gonna Be Happy

Writer: Ray Davies

Lead Vocalist: Ray Davies

A non-album single, this sounds like an attempt at the sort of mildly R&B-flavoured pop that Manfred Mann or the Rolling Stones were recording around this time. Their lowest-charting single for some time, this 'only' reached number 11 in the charts, which is about right - it's a decent enough track, but really should have been album filler rather than a single.

Who'll Be The Next In Line

Writer: Ray Davies

Lead Vocalist: Ray Davies

The B-side to *Everybody's Gonna Be Happy*, this is similarly uninspiring stuff - it's as simplistic as many of the early singles without being in any way interesting or exciting.

Set Me Free

Writer: Ray Davies

Lead Vocalist: Ray Davies

The follow-up single to *Everybody's Gonna Be Happy*, this appears to have been written off the back of the Beatles' *A Hard Day's Night* album, albeit with a return to the almost mantra-like simplicity of the band's previous hits. Here Davies is consciously copying John Lennon, with the A minor key, repeated "little girl"s (something that was a regular feature of the Beatles' lyrics at this time but not of the Kinks') and the brief leap into falsetto for the line "You can do it if you try". Merging these features with the style and structure of their previous biggest hit *Tired Of Waiting For You* would have seemed a sure recipe for commercial success, and so it proved, with the track making the top ten in the UK.

I Need You

Writer: Ray Davies

Lead Vocalist: Ray Davies

A crunchy, riffy track with a prominent tambourine part, this is a clear return to the sound of *You Really Got Me* and (especially) *All Day And All Of The Night*, combining a variant on the latter's riff with the same dropping-out before the guitar solo that had worked so well on the former.

It's clearly an attempt at writing to a formula, and not a particularly good one. It's still better than many of the album tracks on *Kinda Kinks*, but it deserved no better than the B-side it got.

See My Friends

Writer: Ray Davies

Lead Vocalist: Ray Davies

The Kinks' next single was a very brave departure. While this keeps to the simple, repetitive style of their earlier singles, it's even more melancholy than *Tired Of Waiting*, and has a homoerotic subtext ("She is gone and now there's no-one left to take her place/She is gone and now there's no-one else/'cept my friends..."), but it's also the first Western pop record to try to incorporate aspects of Indian music. Davies had heard chanting from river workers during a brief stay in India (hence the otherwise mysterious line about "playing 'cross the river") and had decided to try to write something like that.

The Davies brothers' guitars, detuned and with feedback, are given a vaguely sitar-ish feel here, but it's far from the overuse of the instrument that would become endemic within a year - this isn't cultural appropriation or Orientalism, just an attempt to get a new sound out of their own instruments. As such, it's less embarassing, and less dated, than most of the attempts at incorporating Indian sounds that followed it. The single reached number 10 in the UK.

Never Met A Girl Like You Before

Writer: Ray Davies

Lead Vocalist: Ray Davies

While it starts with a little musical joke (the first couple of bars of *Tired Of Waiting For You*), this track quickly goes into an arrangement similar to that of the band's version of *Beautiful Delilah*. The song itself is utterly nondescript, being based around a twelve-bar blues with repetitive lyrics, and is also utterly forgettable. It was the B-side to *See My Friends*.

A Well Respected Man

Writer: Ray Davies

Lead Vocalist: Ray Davies

And suddenly, the Kinks have turned into the Kinks.

This track and the three following it are from the *Kwyet Kinks* EP of acoustic-flavoured tracks, released in September 1965 (although this track was also released as a single in the US, reaching number 13) and this track in particular sounds like the work of a completely different band. While it's no more sophisticated harmonically than any of the previous material (it's mostly based around a single chord, but with a descending bassline turning that chord from C to C/B to Am - a trick Davies would use again quite often), Davies has learned the secret of writing melodies for his limited vocal range, and the harmonies by Dave Davies on the choruses are worlds away from his caterwauling on the first album.

But it's the lyrics to this which suddenly take a sharp turn for the better. While previously the lyrics to Ray Davies' songs would mostly consist of one or two sentences, repeated over and over, this is a biting, cynical pen-portrait of a member of the upper-middle (or lower-upper) classes, full of a joy at wordplay we've never seen from him before - "And he plays at stocks and shares, and he goes to the regatta/He adores the girl next door cos he's dying to get at her".

And here's where Davies becomes a really good singer as well. He's never been the most rangey or versatile of vocalists, but here he finally learns that he's good at taking on personas and singing in different characters, and the contortions he makes some of the vowel sounds go through when mocking the accent of the "well-respected man" are a wondrous thing to listen to.

This kind of sneering at the businessman in his suit and tie would quickly become tiresome, as every band of the time took it upon themselves to mock the squares, with their jobs and their houses and their responsibilities, and it would often mar Davies' own later work, particularly when coupled with his increasing conservatism. But here it's hard to even think about the negative side of this, as it's such an amazing leap forward in ambition for Davies. While their next proper album would be something of a step back, this song shows what the band would be doing for the rest of the sixties.

Such A Shame

Writer: Ray Davies

Lead Vocalist: Ray Davies

Another track from *Kwyet Kinks*, this one doesn't really fit the 'kwyet' style of the EP, being another repetitive, electric-guitar, simple track. Not particularly inspiring.

Wait Till The Summer Comes Along

Writer: Ray Davies

Lead Vocalist: Dave Davies

A gentle country track, the opening track of the *Kwyet Kinks* EP, this has a rather hesitant melody and structure, as if Ray Davies was having to hunt around for the shape of the track. Dave Davies turns in a better vocal here than most of his previous ones, but seems a little unsure about the song. This is another song that points the way forward in the band's career, this time being in a style they would return to for the *Muswell Hillbillies* album.

Don't You Fret

Writer: Ray Davies

Lead Vocalist: Ray Davies

The other highlight of *Kwyet Kinks*, this is a waltz-time folk-blues song very much in the style of the Odetta covers from the previous album, but this time the band have fully internalised the style and made it their own.

I Go To Sleep

Writer: Ray Davies

Lead Vocalist: Ray Davies

And here we have the best song Ray Davies ever wrote that the Kinks never recorded. This simple piano demo was used as the basis of a wonderful recording by Peggy Lee. Another waltz-time song, based on similar changes to *A Well Respected Man*, though more complex, this seems to have been an exercise in writing in the style of Burt Bacharach and Hal David (listen especially to the way the stresses on "imagine that you're there" fall - that bit of melody could easily come from a Dionne Warwick record.)

This isn't a perfect song - the scansion on the verses is forced, and the middle eight is weak - but it's an astonishingly sophisticated piece of music for a twenty-one-year-old who had only the previous year been writing *You Really Got Me*. It's an absolutely lovely song, and has rightly become something of a standard, being recorded by everyone from Cher to the Pretenders.

Tell Me Now So I'll Know

Writer: Ray Davies

Lead Vocalist: Ray Davies

Another Ray Davies demo, featuring (like the previous and next tracks) Mitch Mitchell (later of the Jimi Hendrix Experience) on drums, this jazzy minor-chord piece has a vaguely Latin feel, and something of the same flavour as some of the Zombies' tracks of the time, and definitely deserved to be taken further.

A Little Bit Of Sunlight

Writer: Ray Davies

Lead Vocalist: Ray Davies

Another demo, this one sounds like something from an earlier era, like a song that could have been a hit for Adam Faith or Tommy Steele, although it also has a family resemblance to *When I See That Girl Of Mine*. While it's catchy enough, it's definitely easy to see why this one was discarded, and given to another band (the Majority, whose version sounds roughly four parts the Four Seasons to one part Joe Meek, and wasn't a hit.)

There's A New World Just Opening For Me

Writer: Ray Davies

Lead Vocalist: Ray Davies

One of the very best of these demos, this combines the folk and Indian influences that Davies had been playing with at the time, using an Indian-style drone, but in much the same way as Scottish folk music does, and with some very impressive finger-style guitar playing. This song was given to American band the Cascades, but really this acoustic demo is a wonderful recording in its own right, seeming to come from some alternative universe where Davies would go on to join Pentangle.

This I Know

Writer: Ray Davies

Lead Vocalist: Ray Davies

Another folk-influenced demo, this one uses those techniques in a much lighter, more cheerful way, to produce a breezy, romantic trifle. This demo is of fairly awful recording quality, but even here the song cuts through, and it's a shame no professional-quality recording of this track exists.

This Strange Effect

Writer: Ray Davies

Lead Vocalist: Ray Davies

A song written by Davies for Dave Berry, patterned after Berry's previous hit *The Crying Game* to a quite ridiculous extent, this BBC session for *Top Of The Pops* (the Brian Matthew-presented radio show, not the TV series of the same name) is pretty much identical to Berry's hit recording, minus the strings.

Hide And Seek

Writer: Paul Winley & Ethel Byrd

Lead Vocalist: Ray Davies

Another *Top Of The Pops* session rounds out the deluxe edition of *Kinda Kinks*, with this cover version of Big Joe Turner's boogie-woogie classic. It works about as well as all the other covers of classic blues by the Kinks, which is to say not at all.

The Kink Kontroversy

The Kink Kontroversy, the Kinks' third album, was their last in their early 'beat group' mode. While it's a definite improvement on the previous two albums, it's also a step back in terms of Ray Davies' songwriting from the non-album tracks that had recently appeared as singles and EPs. It seems, bizarrely, that Davies was seeing his singles as the place for experiment, while the albums were to be kept as close as possible to a formula. This would change with the next album, *Face To Face*, but here we still have a raw rock group rather than the Kinks as they would become, although the darker, more melancholy tinge to the lyrics is quite pronounced.

The Album

Milk Cow Blues

Writer: Sleepy John Estes

Lead Vocalist: Ray & Dave Davies

The album opener is the only cover on the album, a version of an old blues standard. Happily, it's credited to the correct writer, Sleepy John Estes (most recordings credit Kokomo Arnold, whose recording of the song was more successful than Estes' original), though truth be told there's not much to have written in this collection of floating lyrics.[1] This is actually one of the most successful of the Kinks' blues covers, largely because they completely abandon any pretence of playing the blues and instead turn it into a proto-psych rave-up, something like a three-minute version of Love's *Revelation*, with a very prominent piano part from Nicky Hopkins.

Ring The Bells

Writer: Ray Davies

Lead Vocalist: Ray Davies

This song has one of Davies' loveliest melodic ideas, based around a beautiful acoustic guitar riff tic-tocking between D and Asus4 chords. It's such a nice melodic idea, in fact, that the Rolling Stones used it as the chorus to *Ruby Tuesday* a year later. The later song is better than this one, and more developed - this is still from a period where Davies believes that a two-chord riff and some repeated lyrics are enough by themselves to carry a song - but the similarity is so strong it's astonishing that there appears not to have been a lawsuit.

Gotta Get The First Plane Home

Writer: Ray Davies

Lead Vocalist: Ray Davies

A very simplistic song, this track works better than the song due to its well-thought-out arrangement. Session drummer Clem

---

[1] A 'floating lyric' in the blues is a line that is used in many different songs, for example "don't the moon look lonesome shining through the trees/don't your heart feel lonesome when your baby packs up and leaves" or in the case of this song "don't that sun look good goin' down?/that old moon looks lonesome when my baby's not around".

Cattini[2] uses the kick drum and toms to accentuate the riff, which itself is doubled on guitar and bass, while playing straight fours on a cymbal, while Nicky Hopkins plays boogie trills in the very highest range of the piano. Ray Davies also adds some good, if incongruous, blues harmonica. An example of how unpromising material can still be turned into an adequate record, given the right attention to detail in the arrangement.

When I See That Girl Of Mine

Writer: Ray Davies

Lead Vocalist: Ray Davies

A track that seems to have been written in the style of the Everly Brothers, this would have fit perfectly into the pop landscape two years earlier. Were it not for the prominence of the bass, this could pass for something Mitch Miller would write for Gerry And The Pacemakers or Freddie And The Dreamers, with its four-chord banal chirpy verse. It all falls apart slightly in the middle eight, with some rough double tracking and an ineffective key change, but it's still a catchy enough piece of nothing. Bobby Rydell covered this in the US, which pretty much says it all.

I Am Free

Writer: Dave Davies

Lead Vocalist: Dave Davies

The first sign that Dave Davies was going to become a serious songwriting rival to his brother, this is one of the highlights of the album. The lyrics are sixth-form nonsense, written by

---

[2] Mick Avory had had a falling out with the rest of the band, especially Dave Davies, and barely plays on the album

someone who likes using big words without caring very much if he actually understands what they mean, but musically this seems to be an attempt at sounding like Dylan, with its folk-rocking $\frac{6}{4}$ strum. The thirteen-bar verses sound untutored, but utterly natural, and go well with the lyric about wanting to escape from civilisation and be free.

Till The End Of The Day

Writer: Ray Davies

Lead Vocalist: Ray Davies

A top ten hit in the UK, this barely scraped into the top fifty in the US, marking the start of the time when the Kinks' fortunes in the US took a turn for the worse, after they were banned from performing over there thanks to their violent reputation.

It's also a turning point in another way, being the last of the band's generic pop singles. After this, all the rest of the band's hits would be music that only they could have done.

This is a good thing, as this is musically by far the least interesting of the band's run of sixties hit singles, the only real point of note being the way that while its tonal centre is in F (or possibly Dm), it starts in D major and wanders back there occasionally by having A chords rather than the expected Am.

It's a catchy enough pop tune, but they'd done better before, and would do much better afterwards.

The World Keeps Going Round

Writer: Ray Davies

Lead Vocalist: Ray Davies

Another of the many simple, repetitive songs Davies wrote in this early period, this one appears to have been inspired by the

Beatles' *Ticket To Ride*, sharing with it its broken drum part, clangorous guitar and general world-weariness. It also strongly resembles the Beatles' later *Rain*, which has very similar lyrical sentiments.

That said, this is again a clearly minor work, from a writer who still thinks repetition is the key to success.

I'm On An Island

Writer: Ray Davies

Lead Vocalist: Ray Davies

This is one of the few tracks on the album which points the way forward to the band's later work. An *ersatz*-calypso track driven by acoustic rhythm guitar and piano, this immediately sounds worlds more professional than anything we've heard so far, and the song itself is one of the earliest examples of Davies mocking his own depression, something that would come up again and again over the next few years.

Something that could have been self-indulgent moping (our protagonist is "on an island" because he's alone since his girlfriend left him, and he wouldn't mind being alone if he could just be alone with her) becomes instead a tongue-in-cheek piece of self-mockery, and Davies' vocal here, which could easily have fallen onto the wrong side of the comedy racism borderline, just about manages to remain delightful rather than annoying.

The middle eight, interestingly, bears a strong melodic and syllabic resemblance to that of *So How Come (No-One Loves Me)?*, an Everly Brothers track that similarly straddles the borderline between comedy and angst.

Where Have All The Good Times Gone

Writer: Ray Davies

Lead Vocalist: Ray Davies

This, on the other hand, is an absolute masterpiece, and may well be the first post-modern pop song. Davies here impersonates Bob Dylan in his *Like A Rolling Stone* period to deliver a song that is, in part, a denunciation of the way the simple pop music of a year or two ago was being replaced by more complex, mature, downbeat music, like *Like A Rolling Stone*, the Rolling Stones' version of *Time Is On My Side*, and the Beatles tracks *Help!* and *Yesterday*, all of which are parodied during the course of the song.

Except that the song itself is an example of the very form it's parodying, because it's a lyrically mature, complex song about depression and nostalgia, of precisely the type that was only just becoming possible for pop bands to record.

And this tension is at the heart of the song - it's a song about depression, and the tricks it plays on you. The protagonist is depressed not because of anything in particular, but precisely because he's depressed ("wondering where I've gone wrong/Will this depression last too long?".) While he starts by singing about how much better things used to be, soon he realises that "Yesterday was such an easy game for you to play, but let's face it things are so much easier today" and that he needs bringing down to earth.

Not only that, but the idealised past, the "good times", when described seem anything but - they're obviously self-deceiving recollections ("they always told the truth"), but even so they still manage to sound awful ("didn't have no money", "Daddy didn't have no toys and Mommy didn't meet no boys".)

This tension - this longing for a past which is acknowledged as being mythical and never having really existed, while also trying to push forward in progressive directions that wouldn't have been possible in the past, and self-reflexively commenting on both these tendencies - would become the most important and unique aspect of Ray Davies' songwriting within a couple of years, dominating the band's best three albums, *Something Else*, *Village Green Preservation Society* and *Arthur*. We see it here for the first time, in a song that was only considered at the time to be good enough to be a B-side.

It's Too Late

Writer: Ray Davies

Lead Vocalist: Ray Davies

This, on the other hand, is a very basic country song of a type that could have been written by Hank Williams, but played to a slowed-down Chuck Berry rhythm, but without Berry's swing - it sounds for all the world like a prototype for Status Quo.

Had this been played looser, in a more honky-tonk style, this could have been a very decent little track, but as it is it's a bit flat-footed.

What's In Store For Me

Writer: Ray Davies

Lead Vocalist: Dave Davies

While this song is credited to Ray Davies, it sounds to me far more like Dave Davies' work, both melodically and in its subject matter (the lyric is about wanting to see the future, with lines like "I wish I had a crystal ball", which would fit rather well with the younger Davies' well-known fascination with astrology and the occult.)

Either way, this is a minor track, over almost before it's begun. The one interesting feature here is the rhythm guitar part stabbing on the off-beat, a trick presumably borrowed from the Beatles' *She's A Woman*, and one that gives the track almost a ska feel.

You Can't Win

Writer: Ray Davies

Lead Vocalist: Ray and Dave Davies

And the album finishes with a chugalong R&B riff, one of the band's best attempts at playing Mod style soul music. While this is still unimpressive stuff in itself, the difference in technical competence between this and the work on the band's first album is astounding. From here on out, they were going to be able to turn that competence towards far more interesting material.

Bonus Tracks

Dedicated Follower Of Fashion

Writer: Ray Davies

Lead Vocalist: Ray Davies

The first Kinks single to follow up on the social satire style of *Well Respected Man*, this could almost be part two of that song, but this time attacking, rather than the upper classes, the London fashionable set (although there was a great overlap between the two groups at the time.)

While the song was apparently written as a straight attack, written after an argument (a fashionista had criticised Davies for wearing a comfortable but unfashionable jumper), Davies clearly saw an element of himself in the character. He's later stated that the lines "they seek him here, they seek him there" (taken, of course, from *The Scarlet Pimpernel*) were aimed as much at himself and his desire not to be recognised, as well as his lack of a clear sense of identity, as at the character in the song.[3]

In fact the song played a part in Davies' increasing mental ill-health - he claimed later that people would sing the "oh yes he is" chorus at him in the street, and that in his fragile mental state he believed they were saying they knew who he was better than he did himself.

That said, none of this would have been apparent to listeners at the time, who would have taken the song for what it seems - a witty, playful attack on conformity. The language in the song is beautiful - Davies coined the word "Carnabetian" as an adjectival form of Carnaby (after Carnaby St, the most famous fashion-shopping street in London at the time) and there are some lovely lines like "in matters of the cloth he is as fickle as can be". Davies' vocal is also extraordinary, running through a wide variety of different accents and voices effortlessly.

The song does have a bit of a nasty edge to it, as many of the whole 60s 'attacking conformity' genre did, but at least here Davies is attacking the hip and trendy rather than middle-aged normal people.

One thing that is always said about this song which is a complete nonsense, though, is that it's a 'music-hall' song. While some aspects of the song – Davies' vocal, the lyrical concerns and the call-and-response chorus – do owe a little to music-hall traditions, musically this is a country-folk song. Because of the slight influence of music-hall on this song, it's become a trademark of lazy writing about the group to say that many of their songs were music-hall influenced, when most don't even have this level of influence.

I'll go further and go out on a limb and say the song was

---

[3] This would also make the slight homophobic/transphobic tinge of some of the lyrics seem slightly less offputting - Ray Davies has always been publicly ambiguous about his sexuality, while his brother is openly bisexual. If these lines are aimed at Davies himself, that would take the sting out of the song somewhat.

patterned specifically after Johnny Cash's cover of Lead Belly's *Rock Island Line*. Both songs start with a strummed acoustic guitar, playing the same pattern (slightly stressing the off-beats), then bring in a prominent bassline mostly playing around with firsts and fifths, a similar simple drum pattern, and rockabilly picked guitar (Dave Davies seems to be doing a fairly accurate impression of Luther Perkins, Cash's guitarist.) The parallels aren't exact - *Rock Island Line* starts slow and then builds up to a faster pace, while this track stays at one tempo throughout - but this song as recorded owes at least as much to country blues as it does to the music hall.

Sittin' On My Sofa

Writer: Ray Davies

Lead Vocalist: Ray Davies

The B-side to *Dedicated Follower Of Fashion* was this riff-driven freakbeat 12-bar blues, sounding much like every other London band of the time who had heard a few Stax records. It would have been great to dance to in a Mod nightclub, and it is far more accomplished musically than anything the band had done for their first two albums, but it's still ultimately forgettable (and, at 3:07, rather too long for the few ideas it has.)

I'm Not Like Everybody Else

Writer: Ray Davies

Lead Vocalist: Dave Davies

This track, apparently originally intended for the Animals, was released as the B-side to *Sunny Afternoon*, but has become one of the band's most-loved tracks, mostly for its punkish attitude (it includes another little dig at the competition - "I won't say that I Feel Fine like everybody else".) In truth, though, it's nowhere near the song its reputation suggests. It's a very callow piece of work, and it exalts individuality in the most generic way possible, so that it was perfectly possible for IBM, the apex of corporate responsibility, to use it in a TV commercial.

Likewise, I remember seeing Ray Davies perform this live at Glastonbury, in front of an audience of about twenty thousand people, all singing happily along, in unison. Davies even introduced the song by saying "None of us are like anyone else, are we?" and pointing a mic at the crowd to get them to bellow "NO!" as one. The crowd appeared not to see anything amusing in this, though one hopes that Davies at least was aware of what he was doing.

It's a catchy enough song, but at three minutes twenty-eight it outstays its welcome somewhat.

Mr. Reporter

Writer: Ray Davies

Lead Vocalist: Ray Davies

This is a minor piece, a Dylan pastiche right down to the ridiculously lengthened nasal vowels. It's one of the earliest of that annoying subspecies of song, the whine about what a difficult life it is being a rock star. In this case, Davies is attacking, at inordinate length, reporters who misquote him. Some of it is frankly bizarre - "Why, Mr Reporter, do you like some things more than most?" - and there's an anger to the song that unfortunately means it is lacking in craft. This is a purely relative judgement of course - compared even to the songs the band had been recording three months earlier for the album proper, this is a minor masterpiece - but compared to what Davies was capable of, it clearly falls flat.

The band would return to this song again, for a version with Dave Davies on vocals for a projected solo album, but while that version is an improvement on this, both tracks remained unreleased for good reason.

Time Will Tell

Writer: Ray Davies

Lead Vocalist: Ray Davies

A thinly-recorded outtake that sounds more like a demo than a finished recording, this track is more interesting than much of what made it to the actual album. A fuzz guitar raveup, it points the way to another possible direction for the Kinks' music, a road never travelled. Because this song keeps much of the feel of the first three albums, but with more competent musicianship, and with lyrics that seem to deal very frankly with Davies' increasing depression and feeling that he was an actor playing a role - the chorus starts "time will tell if I'll survive/I'd rather be dead than just pretend I'm alive".

This sounds a couple of years ahead of its time, and could easily have been a garage-psych classic for a band like the Thirteenth Floor Elevators.

And I Will Love You

Writer: Ray Davies

Lead Vocalist: Ray Davies

A rather pretty little track that was never taken any further, this is another of Davies' songs of this period that is based around the repetition of a couple of phrases over and over, and is one of his last songs in that style. It does, however, show the increasing musical sophistication of the band, being based around a bossa nova beat and with a Hammond organ pad that one assumes they weren't taking entirely seriously, but which is still a more adventurous sound than much of what they'd used on record earlier.

Davies here uses the same strange vocal style he uses on *I'm On An Island* - a style that sounds like a caricature of an ethnic accent, except that no accent in the world sounds anything like it. It's an odd style, and one he'll return to at several points in the future, but it works.

All Night Stand

Writer: Ray Davies

Lead Vocalist: Ray Davies

A very hissy acoustic demo, this song seems to have been written as a favour for Shel Talmy - it shares a title with a book Talmy's new publishing company was releasing, and was recorded by a band called the Thoughts on a label Talmy owned.

While catchy, it seems completely tossed-off, and its origin is probably visible in the last lines - "Can't get these people off my back/ten percent for this and that". Davies was becoming increasingly uncomfortable with the number of people, Talmy included, who had business interests in the Kinks but who appeared to have little sympathy for his creative aspirations.

The Classic Pye Albums
(1966 - 1970)

Face To Face

Face To Face is very much a transitional album for the Kinks. It was the first album to consist entirely of songs written by Ray Davies (though Dave Davies has claimed in the past to have written the opener, *Party Line*) and the band's line-up was in transition. Pete Quaife had left the band between the recording of the *Sunny Afternoon* single and its release, though by the time the album was released he had rejoined. John Dalton, his temporary replacement for some of the sessions on the album, would replace Quaife after his second, permanent, exit in 1969.

It was also the first album where Davies fully explored the side of his songwriting that had been played with on *Kwyet Kinks*, and is infinitely better than its predecessors. This is the first Kinks album with no embarrassingly bad tracks – the worst track on here would have been among the best on any of the earlier albums. And the sound is different, too – there are more harpsichords than distorted guitars.

The problem is that this is *so* far ahead of the earlier albums as to effectively be by a different band, and so it doesn't really invite comparisons with those, but with the albums immediately after it – and those albums are as far ahead of *Face To Face* as *Face To Face* is ahead of *The Kink Kontroversy*. The general standard of the album is very high – it's the first Kinks album that makes a completely enjoyable listening experience from beginning to end – but not exceptionally so. There are very few truly outstanding songs here, even as there are no bad ones. In this way, *Face To Face* is probably close to the Beatles' album of the previous year, *Help!*, a similarly transitional album and one where, like this, the band's leader (Lennon in the case of the Beatles, Ray Davies in the case of the Kinks) was going through a severe mental breakdown from the opposing pressures of domesticity and pop stardom.

The Album

Party Line

Writer: Ray Davies

Lead Vocalist: Dave Davies

The album starts off with the song that, of all those on the album, sounds most like the Kinks of old. After the opening telephone ring (a remnant of an early concept for the album that would have the songs linked by sound effects[4]) and "Hello, who is it?" (spoken by Grenville Collins, one of the three managers the band had at the time), the song goes into a fairly straightforward, bouncy, three-chord country rock song, much in the vein of the Beatles' Carl Perkins pastiches, with a lusty Dave Davies vocal.

Lyrically, the song is a simple complaint about having to use a party line (a type of telephone service where several people would have to use the same line, and could, if they wished, listen to each other's calls), though with a little nod towards the gender-ambiguity that the band had been playing with ("Is she big, is she small, is she a she at all, who's on the other end?".) There's also a pleasant pun on the phrase "party line" as in "toeing the party line", with the line "I'm not voting in the next election".

---
[4] According to *The Kinks Are The Village Green Preservation Society* by Andy Miller, part of the 33 1/3 series of books

Musically, it's slightly more interesting. While the verse is straightforward – essentially a twelve-bar in G, but without the normal change to the IV on the fifth bar – and the first half of the middle section is just a shuffle between the I and V in D, the middle section then wanders between the keys of D and G for another nine bars in a rather disjointed way, coming in at seventeen bars total.

This is easily the best opener of any Kinks album so far.

Rosie Won't You Please Come Home

Writer: Ray Davies

Lead Vocalist: Ray Davies

A simple but effective song, featuring only five closely related chords and with a simple verse/chorus structure, this song works because of the emotional honesty behind it. The song is written about the Davies brothers' elder sister Rose, who had emigrated with her husband Arthur (of whom more in a couple of albums' time) to Australia two years earlier, and is a simple plea for her to come back at least for a visit if not to stay for good.

Musically, the main points of interest are the pseudo-baroque harpsichord part by Nicky Hopkins, and the way the vocal is doubled during the minor key chorus sections by what sounds like at least two guitars, the bass and possibly a piano faintly in the mix.

The whole is somewhat reminiscent of the Zombies, who had been having some success with similar keyboard-based minor-key songs, and points the way forward to the baroque pop sound of albums like *Da Capo* by Love.

Dandy

Writer: Ray Davies

Lead Vocalist: Ray Davies

The first of the 'social comment' songs on the album is a jaunty, bouncy part-attack part-celebration of a womaniser who is probably based on Dave Davies, and is catchy enough that it was a massive hit single in Europe, as well as a hit in the US and Canada in a soundalike cover by Herman's Hermits. While Ray Davies sings the song with relish (especially the line "two girls are two many, three's a crowd and four you're dead!") it's a rather minor piece.

It is the first of several songs on this album and around this time, though, to feature sections with a descending scalar bassline under a held chord, something that becomes a minor compositional tic of Davies'. This probably either suggested, or was suggested by, the line "while the cat's away the mice are gonna play", as the bass melody under that section is reminiscent of Three Blind Mice. This subtle integration of musical and lyrical themes is something that most listeners will never notice but which greatly adds to the sense of cohesion of the song, and is a sign of Davies' increasing maturity as a songwriter even on a relatively slight song like this.

Too Much On My Mind

Writer: Ray Davies

Lead Vocalist: Ray Davies

As a song, this is a return to the repetitive, simple style of *Tired Of Waiting* or *See My Friends*, but this rather lovely song about suffering from anxiety is saved from sounding like a throwback by the arrangement, with Nicky Hopkins' skittering harpsichord perfectly evoking the feeling of unwanted thoughts running through the brain, while Rasa Davies adds beautiful high harmonies to her husband's lead. A definite highlight of the album, even if there's less to analyse than some of the other songs.

Session Man

Writer: Ray Davies

Lead Vocalist: Ray Davies

An extraordinarily intricate piece of baroque harpsichord, very much in the style of Bach, links the previous track with this one (in fact I wouldn't be surprised at all to discover it was based on some minor work of Bach's, though it doesn't ring any bells and follows a similar progression to that of the rest of the song[5]), before the band pay a backhanded tribute to its player, Nicky Hopkins. Lines like "No overtime, no favours done, he's a session man" and "he's not paid to think, just play" sound quite harsh, but given how much Hopkins' keyboard contributes to this track, and how universally liked he was by the band, one has to assume they are mostly tongue in cheek.

Rainy Day In June

Writer: Ray Davies

Lead Vocalist: Ray Davies

Easily the strangest track on the album, this is quite unlike anything else Davies - or anyone else for that matter - was doing at the time. Starting with a peal of thunder (another of the leftovers from the linking sound effects idea), and keeping an A pedal in the bass throughout almost the entire song, this has a ponderous, depressing feel as the low A turns half the major cycle of fifths the song is built on into a sequence of minor chords.

The lyrics, though, are what makes this really different. This is a dark, impressionist series of glimpses of a fantasy world

---

[5] It's very similar to Prelude No 2 in C minor from the Well Tempered Clavier, but it's not identical.

under some kind of attack - "The demon stretched its crinkled hand and snatched a butterfly/The elves and gnomes were hunched in fear too terrified to cry". It's utterly different from everything else on the album, and from everything else in 1966. One suspects it's a picture of Davies' mental state at the time.

A House In The Country

Writer: Ray Davies

Lead Vocalist: Ray Davies

Sung by Ray Davies in a hoarse voice that sounds almost more like his brother Dave than his normal singing voice, this is one of three songs on this album which appear to be about the same character (who may be at times a cruel caricature of how Davies saw himself at his worst), who is defined entirely by his possession of a large house.

Each of those songs are sung, though, from a different viewpoint, and in this almost proto-punk attack, staying on three chords for almost the entire song, we have the character as seen from the viewpoint of an envious outsider who's "gonna knock him off of his throne".

Holiday In Waikiki

Writer: Ray Davies

Lead Vocalist: Ray Davies

An amusing trifle, this simple ditty starts out with vaguely 'Hawaiian' sounding music (Sandy Nelson-esque drums, ocean sound effects) but soon becomes a typical Kinks track of the period, only the 'Eastern' bent notes on the lead guitar suggesting anything exotic.

Which makes sense, because the song itself is a satire about how the truly different has been packaged, neatened and commercialised, so a holiday in Waikiki now consists of PVC grass skirts, overpriced ukuleles, shacks selling Coke and hula girls from New York. Reducing the Hawaiian elements to a couple of signifiers but otherwise just ploughing ahead with a straightforward Kinks song makes perfect sense in this context.

This song is unfortunately rather spoiled by a bad mix – one of the few on this album that sounds like the bad mixes producer Shel Talmy had inflicted on the earlier albums – with the vocal almost inaudible.

Most Exclusive Residence For Sale

Writer: Ray Davies

Lead Vocalist: Ray Davies

The second of our looks at the owner of an expensive home is the weakest of the three. This time our stately homeowner has been bankrupted, turned to drink and been forced to sell the property, and we see him from a neutral perspective, neither attacking nor sympathising. While there's not much to say about this song beyond that, and it's one of the weaker songs on the album, it's still head and shoulders above almost anything on the first three albums, showing just how much Davies' songwriting had advanced.

Fancy

Writer: Ray Davies

Lead Vocalist: Ray Davies

A return to the pseudo-Indian sound of *See My Friends*, this has a hypnotic, dronelike effect thanks to the repetitive guitar part and sliding bass, and one of the best of Davies' simple, repetitive melodies.

The lyrics are quite extraordinary, seeming to be simultaneously about longing for connection to other people ("if you believe in what I believe in then we will be the same always") and pride in keeping distance from those same people ("they only see what's in their own fancy".) This is wrapped up in the narrator's mind with sexuality, of an ambiguous nature ("no-one can penetrate me" being the crucial line, but also "my love is like a ruby that no-one can see, only my fancy".)

It's not a song that submits well to analysis, but it's one of the most gorgeous, strange songs Davies ever wrote, fading away on a haunting note that sounds like nothing so much as a didgeridoo.

Little Miss Queen Of Darkness

Writer: Ray Davies

Lead Vocalist: Ray Davies

Another fairly minor track, but one that nonetheless shows the skill with which Davies was now able to blend fairly nuanced character studies with music of a wide variety of genres. In this case we have a rather poignant portrait of a woman with something missing in her life after the man she loved left and turning to hedonism, set to a pastiche of 1920s pop music.

The most interesting feature of the track is actually a mistake – in the instrumental break, the instruments fall in and out of sync with each other. Mick Avory has said[6] that this was because he recorded the drum part in the break as an overdub, and Shel Talmy wouldn't let him do a second take, saying it was good enough. The sound of the band drifting out of sync, only to come back together before the next verse, is actually much

---
[6]In an interview at http://kastoffkinks.co.uk

more impressive than it would have been had Avory played the part as he intended.

You're Lookin' Fine

Writer: Ray Davies

Lead Vocalist: Dave Davies

A rather dull, plodding track, the only one on the album that could easily have fit on the first three, this song is based on a bass riff half-way between *Money* and *Peter Gunn*, but not as catchy as either, and the only musical point of interest is a change to a ♭VII where normally one would expect a V. The lyrics, meanwhile, are just about seeing a woman and telling her she's looking fine.

Sunny Afternoon

Writer: Ray Davies

Lead Vocalist: Ray Davies

And tying all the themes of the album together, both musically and lyrically, we have this, one of the band's biggest and best hits. Starting with a descending bass scale in D minor under two chords, recalling the more interesting use of bass in tracks like *Rainy Day In June* and (especially) *Dandy*, the track is in the style that rock music critics usually refer to as 'music hall', despite having absolutely no resemblance to actual music hall music, a sort of laid-back, loose-swinging feel based on strummed acoustic guitar and barrelhouse piano.

The lyrics once again refer to a rich man slowly becoming dissolute, though this time they're sung from his point of view (and Davies is writing at least partly about himself and his newly-rich rock star peers), as he bemoans the taxman taking his yacht away (at the time the top marginal rate of income tax was 95%. This was not very popular with rock stars, who had generally been very poor until recently and didn't like their money going now that they had some.)

The song is wonderfully good-humoured and catchy, and Davies is self-aware enough that it is targeted more at Davies himself than at anyone else – the protagonist here is complaining, but knows he has no real problems. It deservedly got to number one, and is still one of the band's most loved songs.

I'll Remember

Writer: Ray Davies

Lead Vocalist: Ray Davies

Unfortunately, rather than end with *Sunny Afternoon*, which perfectly sums all the album's themes, *Face To Face* ends with this track, which belies its name by being an utterly unmemorable piece of standard early-60s pop, a throwback to 1964 with a simple I-IV-V jangly verse. It's not a bad track, but other than *You're Looking Fine* it is the weakest, and it's a bathetic closer.

Bonus Tracks

Dead End Street

Writer: Ray Davies

Lead Vocalist: Ray Davies

Musically very similar to *Sunny Afternoon* in style, this dark minor-key piece, with its prominent trombone part, could almost be the dark flip of the Beatles' *Penny Lane*, but came out several months earlier than that track. A grim, haunting piece of social comment, it sadly still rings true today – lines like "I'm deep in debt now, it's much too late/We both want to work so hard but we can't get the chance" have only increased in relevance over the years.

Accentuating the feeling of helplessness and being stuck in a dead end, in the chorus the bass (played by Dave Davies on a standard bass and John Dalton on a Danelectro, a technique probably picked up from the records of Phil Spector and Brian Wilson, both of whom did this on many occasions to have an especially thick bassline) keeps playing a four-note descending riff, but it starts on the third note, so it goes from F# down to F, jumps back up to A, then G, then repeats over and over, while the notes in the top of the chord stay essentially the same (the progression is D7/F#-F-Am-Am/G, so there's an A and a C in the chord throughout the chorus.) The feeling we get is of being stuck in one place, going round and round trying to find a way out but always ending up back at the start – a feeling only amplified by the fact that the entire last half of the song is made up of repetition of this musical material, with few words other than "dead end street".

While Shel Talmy is the credited producer, Ray Davies actually produced this himself – unhappy with Talmy's production of the single he took the band back into the studio and rerecorded it with a radically different arrangement. Reportedly when Talmy heard it he couldn't tell the difference.

Remarkably for a song with such a grim message, this went to number five – and would probably have been even more successful had the BBC not refused to show the promo film for it. A pioneering example of music video, this was a wonderful mixture of Eisensteinian bleakness and broad pantomime comedy, apparently supervised by Ray Davies himself, which centred around a troupe of undertakers taking a corpse away from a terraced house[7].

---

[7] A *World In Action* documentary on bronchitis from 1965 opened with shots which look almost identical to some shots from the video –

By this point, the Kinks were at their peak – everything they released for the next four years or so would be wonderful.

Big Black Smoke

Writer: Ray Davies

Lead Vocalist: Ray Davies

The B-side to *Dead End Street*, it shows how far the band had progressed that this was B-side material, as at any point before 1967 it would have been at least considered as a single. As it is, it's a very good minor track, based around a bouncy country rhythm, with yet another descending chromatic bassline with a stationary chord on top (this time the Em - Em/D# - Em/D - Em/C# - C7 that opens the verse and the Em - Em/D# - Em/D - Em/C# that ends it), and another bleak social commentary lyric, this time about the plight of homeless runaways. The subject of homelessness was clearly in the air at the time – I'd initially thought this was inspired by *Cathy Come Home*, but while researching this I found that *Cathy Come Home* was broadcast only two days before this song's release.

The song begins and ends with another of the examples of *musique concrete* style effects that Davies had been experimenting with – church bells at the beginning, joined by the sound of town criers at the end.

This Is Where I Belong

Writer: Ray Davies

---

it would be very surprising if that documentary hadn't influenced both the *Dead End Street* video and the Monty Python sketches which are often pointed to as being similar to it. At the time of writing a clip from this documentary can be found at http://www.youtube.com/watch?v=tW6L9oqnr4M&feature=player_detailpage#t=575s

Lead Vocalist: Ray Davies

The B-side to *Mr. Pleasant*, this sounds like an attempt to write in the style of Bob Dylan's *Highway 61 Revisited* album – it's a very harmonically simple song, built around guitar arpeggios and a Hammond part that sounds almost exactly like the arrangements Dylan was using, and Davies practically does a Dylan impression on the middle eight.

Lyrically, it's just a simple, touching love song. Nothing hugely special, but easily good enough to have been many other bands' A-side at the time.

She's Got Everything

Writer: Ray Davies

Lead Vocalist: Ray Davies

An unsuccessful attempt at a dance song, this is by no means bad as such, but it's a throwback to their earlier work. The fact that even the band were unimpressed can be seen by its release history – while it was recorded during the *Face To Face* sessions, it was left off that album and the subsequent two, before being released as the B-side to *Days* two and a half years after it was recorded. Still better than most of the band's 1964-65 work, it's uninspired and uninspiring.

Something Else By The Kinks

Something Else is the Kinks' first masterpiece. Recorded while Ray Davies was twenty-two, and Dave Davies only nineteen, it's an astonishingly mature album by any standards. When one realises it's only three years since this band were recording mediocre blues covers, the rate at which the band were growing as artists becomes absolutely flabbergasting.

This growth was not, however, without its problems. Pete Quaife had already quit the band and rejoined once, but was becoming increasingly annoyed by Ray Davies' autocratic attitude and paranoia – Davies had taken to making the band rehearse for recordings, and work out arrangements, without hearing his lyrics or vocal melodies in case they would tell his ideas to other musicians who would steal them.

Ray Davies was himself feeling confined by the band and the hit-making formula – after dumping Shel Talmy, the producer of the first four albums, halfway through the recording of this album, and becoming producer himself, he was looking across the Atlantic to the example of Brian Wilson, who would write, produce and sing on the Beach Boys' records but would then send the rest of the band on tour without him. There were plans for both Davies brothers to release solo albums – and indeed three tracks from this album were released on Dave Davies solo singles - *Death Of A Clown* backed with *Love Me Till The*

Sun Shines, and *Funny Face* as the B-side to non-album single *Susannah's Still Alive*. The plan seems to have been that the Kinks would have become Dave Davies' backing band, while Ray Davies would make solo concept albums.

That plan never came to fruition, and despite the difficulties, *Something Else* became the first of a run of studio albums that is equal to any in popular music. It is as far above *Face To Face* as that album was above *The Kink Kontroversy*. This album, more than any other, hit a perfect balance between commercial success (with three hit singles) and artistic achievement. It was, however, the band's worst-charting album up to that point, and would be the last album the band made ever to hit the UK charts at all.

The Album

David Watts

Writer: Ray Davies

Lead Vocalist: Ray Davies

The album starts with the most recognisable opening of any Kinks album, Ray Davies' "nice and smooth" before the count-in to this song[8].

While it's ostensibly about a schoolboy, David Watts was in fact a real person – a concert promoter in Rutland, who had once tried to buy Dave Davies from his brother for his own sexual uses. Once one knows that, lines like "And all the girls in the neighbourhood/Try to go out with David Watts/They try their best but can't succeed" and "He is so gay and fancy-free" become not so much a gay subtext as outright gay text.

---

[8]"Nice and smooth" has taken on its own life in pop culture, becoming a catchphrase of King Mob in Grant Morrison's comic series *The Invisibles*.

Musically, it's a straightforward rocker, all on major chords and for the most part staying on the single chord of D. It's a much better thought-out arrangement, and much tighter playing, than the earlier rockers, though, and is the first example of the two strands of the Kinks' songwriting – the lighthearted social comments and portraits of odd individuals, and the hard rocking riff-based songs – coming together into a cohesive whole.

While this was never released as a single by the Kinks, the Jam had a hit with a soundalike cover version in 1978, which has led to this song appearing on many compilation albums and being one of the Kinks' best-known album tracks.

Death Of A Clown

Writer: Dave and Ray Davies

Lead Vocalist: Dave Davies

While this song's composition is credited to both Davies brothers, this astonishingly mature song is actually the first time that Dave Davies had equalled his brother's songwriting ability, with Ray Davies' only contributions being the "la la la" bridge (sung by Rasa Davies) and the introduction (played on the plucked strings of a piano, and possibly inspired by the Beach Boys' *You Still Believe In Me*, which started very similarly.)

Musically, this is as Dylanesque as the Kinks ever got – simple chords, played on an acoustic guitar, with hoarse, almost sneering vocals – although Nicky Hopkins' barrelhouse piano provides a feeling of continuity with the band's other records from around this time. Lyrically, though, it's a remarkable self-portrait from a young man who was increasingly unable to cope with the alcohol- and drug-fuelled life he was living.

It's also a remarkable vocal *tour de force*, showcasing not only Dave Davies' own voice (a very limited instrument, but expressive when used correctly as it is here) but also Ray Davies' ability to take on other voices (in his wonderfully sarcastic backing vocals), and Rasa Davies, the Kinks' in-studio secret weapon.

This was released as a solo single by Dave Davies, and reached number three in the charts, but Dave Davies soon found the pressure to write follow-up hits unbearable, and while he released several more solo singles over the next couple of years, he didn't start a real solo career until 1980.

Two Sisters

Writer: Ray Davies

Lead Vocalist: Ray Davies

One of the most beautiful songs Ray Davies ever wrote, this is a simple harpsichord-driven song about two sisters, one of whom is living a domesticated life with a husband and children, while the other is living a glamorous life of nightclubs and parties. Davies himself was having very conflicted feelings about his own life as a husband and father, in comparison to his brother's more exciting lifestyle, but seems at least at this point to have accepted his life – the ending of the song, with Priscilla seeing her children and remembering the rewards of her own life, "so she danced round the house with her curlers on, no longer jealous of her sister", is one of the most touching images Davies ever came up with.

No Return

Writer: Ray Davies

Lead Vocalist: Ray Davies

This rather lovely bossa nova track is in many ways the culmination of the fascination with descending chromatic scales seen in several songs on *Face To Face*. Whether it's the D-C#-C guitar parts over C and B♭ chords at the beginning, the way the chord pattern over the line "passed me by" is repeated a semitone lower for "said farewell", or the way the middle eight's chord sequence ends with F-E-E♭-D, the whole backing track is built around a motif of descent by semitones, even as the melody soars upwards.

This lends a harmonic sophistication to the track that is rare in Davies' work, but which suits the genre perfectly (Jobim, the master of bossa nova composition, often tried to fit all twelve notes in the chromatic scale into his songs.) The lyrics, about the loss of one's first real love, are so melancholy compared to the light sweetness of the melody and backing track that the song is lent a wistfulness that is rarely heard in pop music.

The track isn't perfect – some of the acoustic guitar playing is a little hesitant – but this is the fourth minor masterpiece in a row on the album.

Harry Rag

Writer: Ray Davies

Lead Vocalist: Ray Davies

After three rather dark, melancholy tracks in a row, we see here a return to the simpler, more bouncy feel of much of *Face To Face*, with a simple three-chord strumalong about the simple pleasure of smoking a cigarette. A variety of characters are portrayed, facing such eternal enemies as death and taxes with a smile, because they can smoke. Nowhere near as deep or powerful a track as the earlier songs on the album, this is nonetheless a fun singalong.

Tin Soldier Man

Writer: Ray Davies

Lead Vocalist: Ray Davies

This is another throwback to *Face To Face*, and a less successful one. It seems very much to have been written to a formula – simple verse with very few chords, bridge with yet another descending chromatic scale under a stationary chord, lyric mocking conformist city gents... it's the kind of thing you'd come up with were you to try to write a Kinks-sounding song.

It's not without interest – when Rasa Davies' backing vocals come in with the key change to the relative minor on "wicky wack wack oo" the whole track sounds more alive – and it's clearly been worked on. In particular, there are two different sections taking the place of the normal middle eight – the "every day you see his army" and "wicky wack wack oo" sections – showing Davies' love of playing with the boundaries of normal song structure, something that would come out more on *Autumn Almanac*. It's also one of the few tracks on the album to feature instrumentalists other than the four Kinks and Nicky Hopkins – having a small horn section – so may possibly have been considered as a single at one point.

Situation Vacant

Writer: Ray Davies

Lead Vocalist: Ray Davies

Another of the weaker tracks, this little slice-of-life story is essentially a mother-in-law joke writ large – Johnny quits his stable job in order to try to find a better job like his mother-in-law wants, but his mother-in-law gets what she *really* wants when Johnny's wife leaves him because he's got no job at all.

Once again this is musically a fairly straightforward rocker, with yet another chromatic descending bass part (under "for peace and quiet's sake"), suggesting it was tossed off relatively quickly, but it has more imagination than the preceding track, especially in the way Rasa Davies' wordless vocals over the fade merge with the lead guitar part.

Love Me Till The Sun Shines

Writer: Dave Davies

Lead Vocalist: Dave Davies

Released as a Dave Davies solo track as the B-side to *Death Of A Clown*, this was a far less inspired song than its A-side. Other than some very mobile bass playing from Pete Quaife this is the kind of play-in-a-day song most people write once they've learned their first few guitar chords. It's enjoyable enough of its type though, and it shows the quality of this album that even on the third comparatively weak song in a row it's still sounding like the strongest album the band had made til this point.

Lazy Old Sun

Writer: Ray Davies

Lead Vocalist: Ray Davies

Yet another song built around a chromatic descent, this time the whole chord sequence goes down in semitones - F-E7-E♭6-D-D♭7-C7. After me pointing out the overuse of this technique in little spots in some songs on the album, one might expect that I would attack this as lazy. In fact this track, the closest the Kinks ever came to psychedelia (and one suspects a response to the Beatles' *Rain*), is absolutely wonderful, with its low, moaning backwards guitar[9] and throbbing drum part (played exclusively

---

[9] At least, that's my best guess as to what has been done to the guitar sound on the early part of the track. Other people have suggested that it's slowed down to half speed.

on toms and bass drum, with added hand percussion.) Rasa Davies' voice sounds almost like a theremin here, and the whole thing is one of the best group performances on the album, though Ray Davies never thought it came off.

It also has some of Davies' best lyrics, as he sings to the sun "when I was young, my world was three foot seven inch tall/When you were young there was no world at all".

Afternoon Tea

Writer: Ray Davies

Lead Vocalist: Ray Davies

A bittersweet, enjoyable singalong track about the end of an affair, this features some nice country guitar from Dave Davies and a pleasant, simple chorus based around chords descending in whole steps. A lightweight song, but a necessary palette cleanser between two of the densest tracks on the album.

Funny Face

Writer: Dave Davies

Lead Vocalist: Dave Davies

Other than possibly the final track, this is easily the highlight of the album, and the most emotionally raw thing Dave Davies ever wrote.

I don't normally talk in my music books about the personal lives of the musicians, but it's almost impossible to understand Dave Davies without understanding the central trauma of his life – when he was fifteen, he got a girl named Sue pregnant, and planned to marry her. His mother, however, thought that this would destroy his life, and so lied to him and told him that Sue had told her she didn't love him any more, and that Dave was never to see her or their child. He only finally met his daughter in the mid-1990s.

And so we get this song, where the protagonist is being kept from seeing a woman he loves even though "everything you want was bought with lies", who may be taken from him permanently (she's being kept from him by doctors, and "they say you won't last any longer") and so he has to think of her "walking around in my memory". However, he catches a brief glimpse of her "peering through frosted windows" and can reassure himself that "Funny face is all right".

Davies sings the choruses in a falsetto utterly unlike his normal punkish howl, one that's all the more affecting for being clearly out of his range, and these choruses, with their organ and Rasa Davies' almost choral backing vocals, have a hymnal quality that is utterly beautiful.

This was released as the B-side to Dave Davies' solo single *Susannah's Still Alive*.

End Of The Season

Writer: Ray Davies

Lead Vocalist: Ray Davies

Noel Coward had become an influence on Ray Davies' songwriting during the writing of *Face To Face*, and this is possibly Davies' finest pastiche of Coward, down to a perfect imitation of him vocally. Musically, the song places a rather odd basic chord sequence (starting with G then moving to G#, back to G and then to E) against a bassline that moves from the tonic of whatever key the chord implies, to the superdominant, to the leading tone then back to the superdominant, a repeating 'arch' figure similar to some of those used in the Beach Boys' *Pet Sounds*.

The song perfectly follows pre-rock song structure, down to the use of an introduction using separate-but-related musical material from the rest of the song (in pre-rock music this would be called the 'verse', but that word has a different meaning now.) The fun of the song comes from the way Davies juxtaposes this old style against more modern problems like nobody being at the club since a Labour government got in, getting no kicks on Saville Row, and there being no "chicks" around, most of which are concerns one associates more with the Rolling Stones than with Coward.

Of course, now, the gap between 1967 and the present is much larger than the gap between 1967 and the pre-war era Davies is pastiching, and the song takes on a slightly different air, now that Swinging London is further in the past than the British Empire was to Davies.

Waterloo Sunset

Writer: Ray Davies

Lead Vocalist: Ray Davies

There are two types of song I dread when writing about music. The first type is the dull song about which there is nothing much to say – a twelve-bar blues with lyrics like "I love you/yes I do/Ooh it's true" – writing anything at all about such songs is a chore.

But then there are songs like *Waterloo Sunset* (*are* there any songs like *Waterloo Sunset*?), a song so obviously, blatantly perfect, and whose perfection is down to a simplicity and economy of expression, that to analyse it is pointless.

One can point out facts, of course – that Davies originally titled this song *Liverpool Sunset*, that the lead guitar has 50s-style tape echo applied, or that Davies wanted to call the lovers Bernard and Dorothy at first, because Terry and Julie sounded too glamorous – but those facts add nothing to one's appreciation of the track.

And pointing out musical techniques is unnecessary. On some songs, pointing to the change between a minor seventh and an augmented minor seventh and how Davies does something similar on *Set Me Free* might give someone a new appreciation for the song. In this case, everyone already appreciates it.

The best I can do, really, is say that if you haven't listened to this song in a little while, you should listen to it again. Listen to the mono version, not the abysmal stereo mix (thankfully both are on the deluxe CD version), and forget all the facts, like that this masterpiece only got to number two in the singles chart behind Brian Poole And The Tremeloes doing a bad cover of a Four Seasons song. Just listen and you'll agree.

Waterloo Sunset's fine.

Bonus Tracks

Act Nice And Gentle

Writer: Ray Davies

Lead Vocalist: Ray Davies

The B-side to *Waterloo Sunset* is the other type of song I dread writing about (though I wasn't thinking of it when I wrote that passage) – it's a twelve-bar blues with lyrics like "Come on baby, hold my hand/Come on baby, understand". It has some nice country guitar, but is basically forgettable.

Mr Pleasant

Writer: Ray Davies

Lead Vocalist: Ray Davies

The B-side to *Autumn Almanac*, but released as a single in many other countries, this is one of the band's very strongest B-sides and appears on many 'best of' compilations. While it's not up to the standards of their A-sides, and seems to have Davies trying to keep to a 'satirical' formula he'd already outgrown, it still has a lot more life in it than many of the other songs of this type, thanks largely to the vaguely 'trad' trombone part and to Nicky Hopkins' barrelhouse piano.

Susannah's Still Alive

Writer: Dave Davies

Lead Vocalist: Dave Davies

Dave Davies' second solo single (though again featuring all the other Kinks) is actually not as good as its B-side, but is still an extraordinarily good song. Once again apparently inspired by the girl he lost when he was fifteen, whose name was Sue, this tells the story of an alcoholic woman who is waiting for a lost love (a soldier, presumably dead) to return, and "wears nothing in her bed at night/She sleeps with the covers down, hoping somebody gets in".

While musically it's simple – driven by a riff that's a variant on a standard boogie bassline, with vaguely Dylanesque harmonica from Ray Davies, and only four chords – it's a far better song than one would expect from someone as young (and, frankly, thuggish) as Dave Davies was at the time. That it only got to number twenty in the charts is probably due to the slightly garbled lyric (the opening line is "Oh, Susannah's bedraggled, but she still wears the locket round her neck", in case you wondered) and bad double-tracking.

Autumn Almanac

Writer: Ray Davies

Lead Vocalist: Ray Davies

This may be the best single the Kinks ever released, and it's certainly the most complex, despite its singalong sound.

Lyrically, the song is a portrait of a hunchbacked gardener Ray Davies employed at the time, who had scared him as a child and for whom he felt a great deal of empathy (Davies had damaged his back as a child, and has had to take pain medication for most of his life, and he worried for most of his teenage years and early adulthood that this damage would lead to him becoming hunchbacked.) The description of someone living their entire life in one area, watching the football, having Sunday lunch and going to Blackpool for their holidays might sound mildly contemptuous, until one realises that Davies himself has lived almost his entire life within a mile or so of his childhood home and went to see every Arsenal home game around this time. (And Pete Quaife was quoted around this time as saying "LSD seemed to close minds into little boxes... The Kinks all agree that Sunday dinner is the greatest realisation of heaven".)

And here we get to the heart of Ray Davies' writing in this period, which is that he is someone who has always felt attached to his family and local area, and felt a responsibility to them, even as he was having experiences that took him away from anything that could be offered by a pub in Muswell Hill. He disliked himself for getting above his station even as he resented the normality he wanted but couldn't have.

Musically, this is quite astonishingly structured. It's based around the simplest, most obvious chord pattern in music, a cycle of I-IV-V-I (or I-vi-V-I, its close relative), but by moving through different keys (usually by playing with major/minor relations) and time signatures it becomes quite bewildering. To break it down:

We start with an intro, cycling through IV-V-I in E repeatedly, for three bars of $\frac{4}{4}$ followed by one bar of $\frac{6}{4}$.

We then have the first verse, which starts with an Am, rather than the A major chord we would expect. This is the start of a vi-V-I sequence in G, after which the verse plays around with I, IV and V chords in G, and then the whole thing repeats. This is a total of two six-bar sections in $\frac{4}{4}$.

Then there's the section starting "Friday evening...". This starts with Em (in the key of G) but then switches to E major, going back to the key we started the song in. This section goes i-I-IV9-V7-I-IV9-V7-I, a similar pattern to the intro, and consists of one bar of $\frac{4}{4}$, one bar of $\frac{3}{4}$ and four bars of $\frac{4}{4}$.

We then, on the line "Tea, and toasted..." switch to a strange between-keys zone for six bars, before going into the second verse.

The second verse is structured the same way as the first, but has an extra $\frac{6}{4}$ bar of D at the end before going into the next section.

The "I like my football" section is the simplest, just being on the I, IV and V chords of G, the same key as the previous section, and lasting a standard eight bars.

We then have the "this is my street" section, which starts with a key change from G to Gm, but over its eighteen bars (all in $\frac{4}{4}$, but with the bass sometimes implying that they should be split into twos and sixes) wanders in a no-man's land between G, Gm and E, never quite settling on any of them.

Verse three, the last verse, is the same as the first two verses, except that instead of ending "it's my autumn almanac" it repeats "yes, yes, yes, yes" twice (over IV-V-I-V changes) before a coda which cycles through IV, V7 and I in $\frac{6}{4}$ time.

This is a structure that doesn't really admit of any analysis. Rather it's the kind of structure that can only be created by someone who has internalised every lesson of pop song construction so thoroughly that he can ignore any of the rules that get in the way of what he wants to do and know it will work. That it sounds so casual, so effortless, is the true miracle of this song. Contemporaries were making music that was perhaps more complex, but where the Beatles, say, saved a song like *Happiness Is A Warm Gun* for an album track, this was released as a single and got to number three. A truly dazzling, breathtakingly good single.

Good Luck Charm

Writer: Spider John Koerner

Lead Vocalist: Dave Davies

A nice little oddity, this – a cover version of a ragtime-blues song originally released under the name *Good Luck Child* by Spider John Koerner, a Minnesota-based blues revivalist who was friends with (and an influence on) Bob Dylan. For this recording, done for a Dave Davies solo BBC session, Davies and Nicky Hopkins recast it as a Cockney knees-up.

Little Woman (backing track)

Writer: Ray Davies

Lead Vocalist: None

An absolutely gorgeous instrumental, with mellotron[10] on flute setting, chorded piano and a very prominent, melodic bass line. This sounds at times like the Zombies' *Odessey And Oracle*, at times like the Beach Boys, and at times it points forward to ideas that Davies would use on the Kinks' next studio album, *The Kinks Are The Village Green Preservation Society*. This really should have been taken further.

---

[10] A sort of primitive synthesiser, mellotrons were keyboard instruments that had a bank of tapes inside them, of different instruments playing every note. If you put it on, say, the flute setting and pressed middle C, a tape of a flute playing middle C would be heard. Mellotrons were very popular with British bands around this period, and probably the most famous example is the introduction to *Strawberry Fields Forever* by the Beatles.

Sand On My Shoes

Writer: Ray Davies

Lead Vocalist: Ray Davies

This is an early attempt at *Tin Soldier Man*, with the same melody line and a very similar arrangement, with a lyric about being poor but happy, sitting at the beach. The subject (leaving city life behind to escape and live a more relaxed life) is one that Davies would return to, but the lyric here is half-baked at best, and the faked ending doesn't do the song any favours. It's easy to see why he rewrote it.

The Kinks Are The Village Green Preservation Society

The Kinks Are The Village Green Preservation Society is the album that is nearly universally acknowledged as The Kinks' masterpiece, having a thematic and musical coherence greater than any of their earlier albums, while having stronger songs than any of the later ones. It's all the more surprising, then, that such a coherent album had such a tortured genesis.

During the recording of the *Face To Face* album, Ray Davies had written, and the band recorded, a song called *Village Green*, with a nostalgic feel that was quite out of place with the satirical style of that album. He had discussed doing a solo concept album based around the song during the *Something Else* sessions, at the same time Dave Davies' solo career seemed to be taking off, but after a chance remark that the Kinks' music was about 'preservation', the concept for an album about nostalgia gelled, and Davies quickly wrote the title track.

However, the album still had a major hiccup – which is one reason why, happily, there are so many extra tracks from this period. Originally, Ray Davies compiled two albums, one for the European market entitled *The Kinks Are The Village Green Preservation Society*, with twelve tracks, and one for the US, *Four More Respected Gentlemen*, with eleven. But after masters had been created for these, and promotional copies sent out, Davies rethought the album. He wanted to make it into a double album, but the budget-conscious Pye records wouldn't allow him to, and after pushing back the release date by months the final fifteen-song album was released in both the UK and the US.

The album sold pitifully, partly because of the lack of any hit singles on the album, partly because of the release date changing (so all the promotional work was done months before the album itself came out) and partly because the gentle, pastoral sound didn't fit with the psychedelic hard rock that was having success at the time (though 'getting our heads together in the country' would soon become a favoured pastime for rock musicians, and this album now sounds ahead of its time, rather than behind it.)

The Kinks would never have a UK charting album again, and this album marked the end of the hit-making team that had created their unbroken run of classic singles. It was the first album to be wholly produced by Ray Davies, rather than Shel Talmy, and it was the last album on which bassist Pete Quaife played, before he left the band forever in fairly acrimonious circumstances. It was also the last Kinks album to feature keyboard player Nicky Hopkins, whose mastery of a wide range of styles had added so much to the Kinks' sound. Hopkins was enraged when the album came out to find that Ray Davies (who played a small amount of keyboards on the album) was credited as "guitarist, keyboard player and singer", while Hopkins wasn't even credited as among those who 'contributed'. Hopkins refused ever to work with the band again, and claimed for the rest of his life that he'd never even been paid for his work on the album.

However, the album has in recent decades been critically reappraised, and it is now among a select group of albums (also including *Forever Changes* by Love and *Odessey And Oracle* by the Zombies) that are considered essential albums of the 60s even though they sold almost nothing on their release. The Kinks' biggest flop up to that point now comfortably outsells the rest of their catalogue and regularly makes "best album of all time" lists.

It's also the album that has had the most lavish reissue. All the Kinks' 60s studio albums are currently available in double-CD versions with mono and stereo versions of the album plus bonus tracks, but *The Kinks Are The Village Green Preservation Society* is available as a three-CD set, and so there are more tracks for us to look at here than on any other Kinks album.

The Album

The Village Green Preservation Society

Writer: Ray Davies

Lead Vocalist: Ray Davies

The title track of the album was written and recorded fairly late in the album's genesis, and seems to have been written quite quickly once Davies had the inspiration. The backing track is just I-V-IV-V chords throughout, first in C and then (from "We are the Sherlock Holmes English Speaking Vernacular") in D, apart from a single change to III on the last line of the choruses, while the lyric seems to have been written with the aid of a thesaurus (every alternate line in the verses ends with a synonym for 'society', except the Sherlock Holmes line — clearly his thesaurus was rather unreliable.)

That said, there's a more serious point to be made by this song, and indeed by the whole album. 1968, the year of the album's release, was a year of political ferment, though much less so in the UK, where people were able to take a somewhat detached view of proceedings, than in the USA, where young men were being sent off in their thousands to kill or be killed, or in Czechoslovakia, which had been invaded by the Soviet Union.

Youth culture generally was on the side of revolution, and while a few rock stars managed to sit on the fence about the idea (notably John Lennon with *Revolution*), most were expected to pay at least lip service to the idea. But the Kinks were an altogether more conservative band. Three weeks before this album was released, the White Panther Party had released their manifesto calling for "Total assault on the culture by any means necessary, including rock 'n' roll, dope and fucking in the streets." The Kinks, on the other hand, were calling for vaudeville, draught beer and virginity.

The Kinks couldn't have made a more blatant declaration of their irrelevance to the times they were living in if they'd tried, but by doing so they managed to create an album that is timeless.

Do You Remember Walter

Writer: Ray Davies

Lead Vocalist: Ray Davies

A beautiful, wistful song, summed up in its last line "People often change, but memories of people can remain", this song is the heart of the album. Inspired by a real person, as so many of Davies' songs are, this finds the universal in the specific. Almost everyone has had a close friend with whom they've fallen out of touch, and who they've later reunited with to find they have nothing in common, but Davies here uses the specifics of his friendship with Walter ("playing cricket in the thunder and the rain?" "We'd save up all our money and we'd buy a boat and sail away to sea") to conjure up the bittersweet emotions of such a friendship far better than a more generic lyric ever could.

The music reinforces this ambiguity – the fondness for the friendship alongside the recognition that the friendship can never exist again — by floating between two keys, C and B♭, a tone apart, meaning that while the song starts out in C, the chord sequence keeps gravitating towards the melancholy Cm7.

Picture Book

Writer: Ray Davies

Lead Vocalist: Ray Davies

One of the more minor songs on the album, Ray Davies thought highly enough of this that it was included on the line-ups of both the 12-song *Village Green Preservation Society* and of *Four More Respected Gentlemen*, unlike the two previous songs which were included on the former but not the latter.

Based around a fairly simple cycle-of-fifths chord sequence for the verses, with a chorus that's just F and C, and a guitar riff that's little more than an ascending chromatic scale, this is once again a song featuring real people from Davies' life, this time describing photos of his parents and "fat old Uncle Charlie" on holiday. The song's jollity almost manages to hide the melancholy tinge that creeps in with lines like "when you were just a baby, those days when you were happy, a long time ago". Certainly when HP used it in a commercial in 2004 they were not, one hopes, intending to imply that for their customers happiness would be a distant memory accessible only through photographs.

Johnny Thunder

Writer: Ray Davies

Lead Vocalist: Ray Davies

One of the weaker songs on the album, this play-in-a-day portrait of a rebel biker who rejects society but is nonetheless prayed for by one of the women in "the town" (most of the songs on this album appear to take place in a common setting, a mythical English village that's deliberately left ambiguous) was inspired by the belated release in Britain earlier that year of the 1953 film *The Wild One*[11], and in particular the character Marlon Brando plays, Johnny Strabler, leader of the Black Rebels Motorcycle Club.

While the song's central character is certainly an individualist, of a type celebrated by many of the songs on the album, the celebration here of a fairly cliched biker type, rebelling in the most obvious manner, seems to lack subtlety when compared with the songs around it.

Last Of The Steam-Powered Trains

Writer: Ray Davies

Lead Vocalist: Ray Davies

This was one of the last songs recorded for the album, being written and recorded after the original twelve-track *Village Green Preservation Society* was pulled from release, and it feels very different from the rest of the album musically, if not lyrically.

Musically, this points the way forward to the harder rock music the band would be doing on their next album, *Arthur* – the song is based around the riff to Howlin' Wolf's blues classic *Smokestack Lightnin'* and has a long instrumental section that makes this the longest track the band had ever recorded to this point, at four minutes ten seconds.

---

[11] Note that while Paul McCartney has claimed that the Beatles were named in part after the Beetles, one of the two gangs in this film, it would have been impossible for any of the Beatles to have seen it until many years after the band formed, as it was banned in the UK until late 1967, and first shown in the UK at a private screening in 1968.

Lyrically, however, the song fits the album perfectly, and helps tie together its twin themes of nostalgia and individualism. Davies takes the train blues (a standard form that was dying out in its home, the US, as the passenger railways were being replaced as a symbol of freedom with the car) and uses it as a basis for a song about remaining (or wishing to remain) working-class and eccentric as one's friends become steadily more middle-class and conformist.

The central metaphor (the narrator comparing himself to a steam trains) is a telling one. Not only were steam trains a thing of the past (the last mainline steam train voyage in the UK having been in August 1968, and this track being recorded in October of that year), being replaced by electric or diesel trains (which don't have the rhythms or horn sounds that inspired the train blues sound), but nostalgia for steam trains was, itself, out-of-date. A few years earlier there had been regular campaigns to save beloved steam trains from being scrapped, but these had stopped getting any publicity, as the replacement of steam had become inevitable.

So Davies here is presenting himself as someone so out-of-step with modern times that even his nostalgia was out-of-date, and as the last rebel in an increasingly conformist society. In fact, he was so out-of-step with the times that he was almost getting back into step, as the blues-rock style of this track would become the norm for many of the newer bands who were becoming popular as the 60s turned into the 70s. But even if it's factually wrong, emotionally this track is enormously resonant. If *Do You Remember Walter?* is the best song on the album, and its emotional core, this is the thematic core of the album, and the basis on which their next one would be built.

A year after its release, this was used as the theme for an episode of *The Wednesday Play* on TV, for a play called *Last Train Through The Harecastle Tunnel*.

Big Sky

Writer: Ray Davies

Lead Vocalist: Ray Davies

While this was, along with *Last Of The Steam-Powered Trains*, one of the last songs recorded for the album, it was actually written some nine months earlier. Andy Miller, in his *33 $\frac{1}{3}$* book on this album, speculates that Davies wanted to keep it for the solo album he was still, in early 1968, half planning.

However, Miller's other claim, that the song doesn't fit the album particularly well thematically, is clearly balderdash. While the song isn't especially about nostalgia or English village life, it *is* about an individual who feels cut off from the rest of society – in this case, about God himself. "Big Sky" in this context is just the ultimate outsider, like Monica or Wicked Annabella or the Phenomenal Cat, looking down dispassionately at the people he would like to care about but for whom he can't be bothered to feel bad.

This dispassionate, objective attitude is seen in the song as something to aspire to, in the most beautiful melodic passage of what is a largely spoken song – "one day, we'll be free, we won't care, just you see". In a world which has a God who doesn't care, the best freedom we can hope for is to not care ourselves. Thus detachment from society, as idolised in the rest of the album, eventually becomes detachment from the self. Given that Davies had had a breakdown shortly before writing the song, one can sympathise with the wish to be free of the stresses of the world, even if in retrospect it looks itself like a symptom of the problems he was having.

Regardless, *Big Sky* is a lovely piece of music, one that actually manages to turn the hope of a future without feeling into a positive, comforting, sharing thought right now. One of the finest things on the album.

Sitting By The Riverside

Writer: Ray Davies

Lead Vocalist: Ray Davies

Side one of the album closes with one of the more minor pieces, and one that was recorded relatively early in the sessions for the album, but left off the initial tracklistings. This is a gentle, pastoral track based around piano and mellotron on accordion setting. The most notable feature of the song is that it is the one nod toward psychedelia on the album – after the lines "I can close my eyes" and "like a willow tree" we get an instrumental freak-out section that sounds a little like the orchestral sections of the Beatles' *A Day In The Life* redone on a budget of tuppence ha'penny, presumably meant to represent a dream state.

Even this, though, one of the least interesting tracks on the album, is only relatively so. The standard of this album as a whole is utterly astonishing, and we close side one without having had a single track that was less than excellent.

Animal Farm

Writer: Ray Davies

Lead Vocalist: Ray Davies

Side two opens with a song which was a favourite for all the band members, even though it caused a row between Pete Quaife and the Davies brothers (Quaife wanted the bassline on the intro to double the piano intro, while the Davies brothers both wanted him to play the more mobile part that ended up on the record.)

An absolutely joyous track, with layers of stacked vocals, treated guitar, tack piano and mellotron on a string setting, this is one of the musically simplest songs on the album – although the album as a whole has seen a retreat from the musical experimentation of tracks like *Autumn Almanac*, and most songs have a fairly straightforward verse/chorus structure and are based around chord changes of a fourth or a fifth – easy, poppy chords. This whole song is based around only four chords in total, E, G, A and D, and has no key changes or real harmonic movement, getting all its effects from changes in tempo and density of arrangement.

The subject of the song, a wish to return to nature and be away from civilisation, is one that Davies would return to throughout his career, but rarely so successfully as here.

On the subject of the title... the song has no connection with the Orwell novel of the same name, but Andy Miller, author of the $33\frac{1}{3}$ book on the album, has suggested that there are a number of parallels between this album and Orwell's early novel *Coming Up For Air*, which would suggest that a link between Orwell's work and this album would merit further investigation.

In truth, though, while there are some similarities – both men prized elements of working-class British life and seemed to seek out some form of authenticity in rejecting middle- and upper-class life even as they made their livings in the arts, both loved an imaginary England (and specifically England, not Britain) that never existed – Orwell would undoubtedly have been very critical of Davies' work. Davies is, like Orwell, essentially slumming when he tries to be working class – his concerns are those of the rich, or, at the very least, those of the insecure middle classes. While he can write affectingly about poverty, he's more likely to attack unions, high tax rates, the welfare state, and other aspects of life which he views as interfering in one's ability to live a life free of others' meddling. Davies' combination of an instinctively libertarian politics with a reactionary worldview would not have been one that Orwell would have let go without comment, however much the two men's aesthetics may seem superficially close.

Village Green

Writer: Ray Davies

Lead Vocalist: Ray Davies

While this track was the inspiration for the entire album, it feels (sonically, if not lyrically) somewhat out of place here. The song is harmonically more mobile than anything else on the album, proceeding in a stately manner through all the major and minor triads in Cm, rather than the simpler sequences we're used to with this album, and in the middle eight we have the old *Face To Face* era standby of having a bassline descending by semitones while we stay on one chord (Fm for four bars, then repeated on Cm for four bars.)

The track is also somewhat tinnier than those surrounding it, possibly suggesting the hand of Shel Talmy in its production, though he is not credited on the album.

But the most striking feature of the track is its arrangement. Nicky Hopkins once again uses the baroque harpsichord style he had used to such great effect on several *Face To Face* tracks, and because this track was recorded when the band were at their commercial height, rather than on a downslide, Pye allowed the band to use a small orchestra.

And the orchestration is dazzling – David Whittaker uses a very small number of instruments to create a sound reminiscent of Purcell, combining an oboe part full of trills and ornamentation, sounding almost crumhorn-like, with a bassoon part that moves in parallel to the oboe before going its own way at points.

The song has a camp archness to it, especially evident in Davies' vocal, that isn't really present on the rest of the album, and for that reason if no other it's a welcome reminder of Davies' wit, otherwise not especially present on this most sincere of Kinks albums.

Starstruck

Writer: Ray Davies

Lead Vocalist: Ray Davies

And after a song that was recorded two years earlier, we come to a song that sounds like it was recorded during the height of the beat boom. Davies' attempt at writing a soul track, this has a hook based on descending chords that sounds very Holland-Dozier-Holland, while the backing vocals on the chorus are a girl-group chant, but with a British band singing it, it inevitably sounds closer to the Beatles' mid-sixties work than to actual soul music.

While this is a pleasant enough track, neither the music nor the lyrics (a warning to a woman who is possibly having too much of a good time, as well as being too impressed by Davies himself) really fit the tone of the rest of the album, so it's quite surprising it was on the original twelve-track line-up of the album.

This was released as a single in the US and parts of Europe, the only single to be released from the album, and made number 13 in the Netherlands.

Phenomenal Cat

Writer: Ray Davies

Lead Vocalist: Ray Davies

One of the band's very rare forays into psychedelia, this strange little nursery rhyme about a cat who "lived to eat, 'cause it kept him fat, and that's how he wanted to stay" hits almost all the standard British psychedelic notes, from the whimsical childlike lyric to the mellotron on flute setting to Dave Davies' varispeeded vocal (sounding uncannily like Bluebottle from the

Goons) on the chorus. If they'd phased something or added a backwards guitar it would almost be the type example of British psychedelia ca. late 1967.

Fortunately, the track is still of interest even on what is otherwise a non-lysergic album. Nicky Hopkins' mellotron part is quite exquisite, and while the story of the phenomenal cat may at first seem childish, it's yet another song about an outsider looking dispassionately at the world around him. In particular, it's notable that for Ray Davies, at least as far as this song goes, the main benefit of going on a pilgrimage and gaining spiritual insight is that if you gain the secret of eternal life you don't have to diet any more. It's precisely that kind of attitude that kept Davies' feet on the ground as a songwriter, while all around him everyone else was writing songs about their great insights.

All Of My Friends Were There

Writer: Ray Davies

Lead Vocalist: Ray Davies

One of the very few Kinks songs to actually show the music-hall influence that lazy writers claim for most of Davies' work, this is a genuinely funny comic song about what must be every performer's nightmare (though it apparently actually happened to Davies) – turning up to do an important show, having a few too many drinks to steady the nerves (Davies is apparently *very* susceptible to alcohol, because of the pain medication he takes for his back), and going on and doing an horrific performance, only to discover that all your friends are sat in the audience watching.

The lurch from the upbeat, jaunty verse into the woozy, drunk, waltz-time chorus, with its descending stepwise bassline this time sounding like someone falling down very, very slowly, is one of the funniest moments in the Kinks' catalogue, with the hyperbolic bathos of "All of my friends were there... not just my friends, but their best friends, too".

This song was, like *Sitting By The Riverside*, recorded quite early in the making of the album but left off the initial track-listings. It's hard to see why, as it's one of the most engaging tracks on the entire album.

Wicked Annabella

Writer: Ray Davies

Lead Vocalist: Dave Davies

This spooky little story about a witch who lives out in the woods is one of the few opportunities on the album for someone other than Ray Davies or Nicky Hopkins to shine, and the rest of the band seize the opportunity with relish. A slow, heavy rocker, it starts with a prominent drum part by Mick Avory, which stays high in the mix throughout. Dave Davies not only gets to play the fuzz guitar riff but also to do a wonderfully sinister vocal, going from the creepy insinuation of the verses to the terror of the "I've seen her face" section, and Pete Quaife actually gets to play a short bass solo, where he shows off by playing a snatch of *Jesu, Joy Of Man's Desiring* in $\frac{4}{4}$ time.

Not one of the best songs on the album, it is still a welcome burst of heaviness in an otherwise very light album side, and shows that however much this may seem like a Ray Davies solo project, the Kinks were still a band and every member was capable of pulling his weight.

Monica

Writer: Ray Davies

Lead Vocalist: Ray Davies

A simple three-chord cod-calypso song, once again featuring Ray Davies' attempt at a Carribean accent (though thankfully toned down a bit compared to some of the horrors he would later inflict in this style), this is a love song written about a streetwalking prostitute.

I'm in several minds about the subject of this song, though I'll keep it brief. To start with, I think it's a genuinely good thing that Davies would write a song about a prostitute which treats her as a human being, rather than purely as a sex object, but on the other hand, I think that there is an element here of what one might look at as the sex worker equivalent of the magical Negro – the prostitute who secretly understands all her clients but is saving her love for just one. On the gripping hand, though, no doubt there are such prostitutes out there...

Either way, the song has a light, enjoyable feel, and while it's not a highlight of the album, it definitely deserves its place.

People Take Pictures Of Each Other

Writer: Ray Davies

Lead Vocalist: Ray Davies

And now we get a song that ties everything together, in a superficially jolly but utterly heartbreaking closing. Here we tie up all the themes – an outsider, looking back at "a time when [he] mattered to someone", the lost happiness of youth, artifacts from the past persisting into a present where their context has changed irrevocably – with the simple plea "Don't show me no more, please".

For all its appeal, nostalgia is ultimately a deadly emotion, because it prevents one moving on, and here, in the closing song, we see an acknowledgement of the rot at the core of that emotion. The photos are only letting the narrator hold on to his bitterness – "you can't picture love that you took from me"

– and he recognises that no matter how unpleasant the present may be compared to the past, he still has to live in it.

The Kinks Are The Village Green Preservation Society is a remarkable, beautiful, astonishing work, one of the great albums of all time. But it's not a particularly pleasant album, or a comforting one, despite the cozy nostalgia of the opening track. Rather, it's an album that shows that an obsession with the past over the present eventually leads to becoming one of the loner characters that are dotted throughout the album, refusing to care about anything in the present day.

It's undoubtedly a masterpiece, but it's easy to see why it wasn't a hit. At a time when childish whimsy was giving place to adolescent rebellion, a work as fundamentally adult as this never could be.

Bonus Tracks

Mr. Songbird

Writer: Ray Davies

Lead Vocalist: Ray Davies

A lovely little minor track that was on the original 12-song *Village Green Preservation Society* as well as *Four More Respected Gentlemen*, but pulled from the final lineup, this wistful, bouncy little mellotron-led track about the joys of music is perhaps not as substantial as much of the rest of the album. That said, it's a sign of how good a band the Kinks were at this point that they could leave material as strong as this unreleased, though it would undoubtedly have made the tracklisting if the proposed double-album version had ever been made.

Days

Writer: Ray Davies

Lead Vocalist: Ray Davies

The last single the original line-up of the Kinks ever released (though Pete Quaife played on one more single, released after he left) was this astonishingly beautiful song, possibly the best thing Davies ever wrote.

The song, apparently about the end of an affair but also (or so Davies now claims) about the break-up of the original line-up of the band, is one of those simple songs that resist all analysis. All the strength of the song lies in its sentiment – a statement to a lover who has left that it's better to have loved and lost than never to have loved at all, and that the happiness she gave was more than worth the sadness of her departure. It's one of a very small number of songs that can regularly move me to tears, and it does so by underplaying, rather than exaggerating, the emotion. A line like "now I'm not frightened of the world, believe me" says volumes about the bravery of the man facing the night alone, about what the nameless person to whom the song is being sung meant to him, and about what his life is going to be like without her, without ever trying to tug on the heart-strings.

There's some evidence that Ray Davies himself didn't realise just how good this song was. Released as a single, it went to number twelve in the UK, but[12] it never entered the Kinks' live set until twenty years later, after Kirsty MacColl had a hit with a cover version. Davies now dedicates the song to MacColl, and to Pete Quaife (who died in 2010) in live performances.

Certainly, while the song was included on the twelve-track version of *Village Green Preservation Society* and on *Four More Respected Gentlemen*, it was dropped from the final version of the album, and left as a single-only release, leaving *Village Green Preservation Society* as the only Kinks album of the 60s not to feature a UK hit single.

---

[12] According to Miller

But now, the song is rightfully considered a pop classic. If the only two songs Ray Davies had ever written had been this and *Waterloo Sunset*, he would still have a good claim to be one of the great songwriters of the twentieth century.

Polly

Writer: Ray Davies

Lead Vocalist: Ray Davies

The B-side to *Wonderboy*, it says something about how good the Kinks were at this point that a song as strong as this was relegated to a B-side.

Dylan Thomas' *Under Milk Wood*, with its description of pastoral village life and cast of eccentrics, was a clear inspiration for Davies' work around the time of *Village Green Preservation Society*, and here Davies takes the name (though nothing else) of one of the characters, Polly Garter, and puns with it on the Pretty Polly brand of tights (from which Thomas may have taken inspiration in the first place) to give himself a chorus, around which he builds another of his tales of a young girl who is corrupted by the big city (though here she goes back home to the chains of her family.)

There's nothing in this song that Davies hadn't done elsewhere, and relatively recently, but it's done exceptionally well here.

Wonderboy

Writer: Ray Davies

Lead Vocalist: Ray Davies

This was the Kinks' first comparative flop since *You Really Got Me*, going only to number 36 in the UK charts. It's hard now to see why, though, as the song itself, with its gentle message of reassurance, is easily as strong as all but the very best of the band's singles to that point.

The song was reputedly John Lennon's favourite Kinks song, with a story often being told that he insisted, on hearing the song while out (either at a club or a restaurant, depending who's telling the story), on having the record played over and over again for the entire evening. It's easy to see why – not only is the song's lyrical message, telling someone who's going through a difficult time that things will be OK, something that would have resonated with Lennon at the time (like *Hey Jude*, which is very similar in sentiment), but the lyric and vocals are Davies at his most Lennonesque (so much so that Oasis, a 90s rock band famed for attempting to sound like the Beatles and failing miserably, stole the "I see you and you see me" section of this song for their hit *She's Electric*.)

All that said, the band themselves apparently detested the track, Pete Quaife later calling it horrible, and Ray Davies saying it should never have been released. It's a shame, because despite its lack of commercial success, this is another great single by a great singles band.

Berkeley Mews

Writer: Ray Davies

Lead Vocalist: Ray Davies

A very good song, loosely inspired by *September In The Rain* (the melody, as well as the lyric, on the line "The leaves of brown came falling through the view" is almost identical to "The leaves of brown came tumbling down, remember", and the structure of the verses is similar), this tale of a one-night stand that ended badly is hamstrung by an overly-busy arrangement, going from honky-tonk piano to boogie bass to a parodic 50s rock ending. It was intended for *Four More Respected Gentlemen*, but whether because of the poor arrangement or because of fears of a copyright infringement lawsuit it remained unreleased until 1970, when it was released as the B-side to *Lola*.

Misty Water

Writer: Ray Davies

Lead Vocalist: Ray Davies

Another song that was intended for *Four More Respected Gentlemen* but was left unreleased, this is another track that, while not quite up to the standards of the tracks that made it to the finished *Village Green Preservation Society*, nonetheless deserved better than the obscurity to which it was consigned.

A song about the pleasures of drunkenness, this works almost entirely in metaphor and allusion, from its opening line "By the town of Straight And Narrow", with a town name worthy of Bunyan, to the title of the song itself, a reference to alcoholic drink.

Parts of the song bear some slight resemblance to some of the musical ideas in *Shangri-La*, from the band's next album, but other than a brief release on the unauthorised compilation *The Great Lost Kinks Album* this remained unavailable until the release of the *Village Green Preservation Society* deluxe edition. A shame.

Easy Come, There You Went

Writer: Ray Davies

Lead Vocalist: None

An utterly unmemorable instrumental, this remained unreleased until the deluxe edition came out. No-one was missing anything much.

Did You See His Name

Writer: Ray Davies

Lead Vocalist: Ray Davies

Around the time of *Village Green Preservation Society* Ray Davies was writing songs, usually on topical subjects, for several TV shows. This one was written for *At The Eleventh Hour*, and was inspired by reading through the newspaper looking for ideas and coming across an obituary for Davies' doctor.

One presumes, though, that the story told here bears little or no resemblance to that of Davies' GP, as it tells a story of a man living in poverty who steals a tin of beans "from a cut-price grocery store", is named-and-shamed in the newspaper, loses his job, and kills himself because he can't live with the shame.

The song is obviously one that was written quickly, rather than crafted over a longer period, and some infelicities remain as a result ("his little job", for example, is clearly just there to fill out the syllables), but it's surprisingly good for a throwaway piece. Certainly Davies must have thought so – it's the only song from his *At The Eleventh Hour* work that the Kinks recorded, and it was intended for release on *Four More Respected Gentlemen*, though it didn't end up getting released until a US-only compilation in 1972.

Mick Avory's Underpants

Writer: Dave Davies

Lead Vocalist: None

A nondescript instrumental, with a prominent drum intro.

Lavender Hill

Writer: Ray Davies

Lead Vocalist: Ray Davies

A pleasant, mellotron-led track with a slight resemblance to some of the Zombies' contemporaneous work, this is one of a very small number of Kinks tracks that could actually be called overproduced. The mellotron, the backwards-recorded backing vocals, the forwards backing vocals, the overly-busy bass line at the end, and the solo (which sounds like a guitar put through a wah-wah pedal and recorded backwards, to my ears) all have decent ideas in them, but clash with each other – and the tape-speed problems inherent in both backwards recording and in using a mellotron mean that everything sounds ever-so-slightly off-key compared to everything else.

There's a nice idea for a song here – you can definitely tell what Davies was going for – but it doesn't quite come off. This was briefly released on *The Great Lost Kinks Album*, but otherwise remained unavailable until the 2004 deluxe edition of *Village Green Preservation Society*.

Rosemary Rose

Writer: Ray Davies

Lead Vocalist: Ray Davies

A rather lovely little piece, based around an arpeggiated piano figure and rough harpsichord, this character piece (presumably written about memories of the Davies' sister Rose) would have fit perfectly on *Village Green Preservation Society*. Oddly, it seems to have been inspired by *You Really Got Me*, as can be heard in the instrumental break, when the harpsichord plays a figure very similar to the *You Really Got Me* riff. Try singing the title of one over the other, and you'll see what I mean. This was another one that was briefly available on *The Great Lost Kinks Album* but then remained unreleased until 2004.

Spotty Grotty Anna

Writer: Dave Davies

Lead Vocalist: None

A dull instrumental blues jam, this was apparently named after a notorious groupie on the London scene.

Where Did My Spring Go?

Writer: Ray Davies

Lead Vocalist: Ray Davies

Another song written for a TV show, this was written for the second episode of *Where Was Spring?*, a sketch show starring Eleanor Bron and John Fortune that was apparently one of the best things on TV at the time. Unfortunately, we'll never know if it lived up to its reputation, because in the same act of cultural vandalism that led to the destruction of the tapes of the TV coverage of the moon landing and of the Beatles' performances on *Top Of The Pops* among many others, the BBC in its wisdom decided to destroy all existing copies of the show to save space.

This recording is little more than a full-band demo, but sketches out a song that fits the mood of *Village Green Preservation Society* very well, even though it was recorded some months after the album's release, with its narrator having been left by a lover who was just using him, and reflecting on his lost youth and health. While these sentiments may seem rather unusual for someone who was, as Davies was when recording this, only twenty-four, it should be remembered that Davies has had poor health for most of his life, so when he sings "Why ain't my back straight? Why do my feet ache?" we can presume he knows what he's talking about.

This is only a trifle, but even the trifles the band were recording at this point were better than many bands' best work. Once again, this was released briefly on *The Great Lost Kinks Album* then stayed unavailable til 2004.

Groovy Movies

Writer: Ray Davies

Lead Vocalist: Dave Davies

By rights, this should have been a bonus track on *Arthur*, having been recorded six months after *Village Green Preservation Society* was released, and it has little to do with the rest of the recordings here. An attempt at horn-driven Memphis soul, with Dave Davies turning in a rather sub-par vocal (more shouted than sung), this is a fairly straightforward track about Ray Davies' desire to be a film director.

King Kong

Writer: Ray Davies

Lead Vocalist: Ray and Dave Davies

This track, a return to the riff-driven rock of the band's early days, was recorded either towards the end of the *Village Green Preservation Society* sessions or several months later – it sounds to me like the latter. A lumbering, distorted hard-rock track with little subtlety about it, but still somehow enjoyable, this was released as the B-side to *Plastic Man*.

Arthur (or The Decline And Fall Of The British Empire)

And so we come to the first Kinks album that could reasonably be considered to be worse than its predecessor.

Which is not to say that *Arthur* is in any way a bad album – in fact its best songs are considerably better than the best material on *Village Green Preservation Society* – but rather that there are just the occasional signs here of an incipient flabbiness, a tendency to extend songs beyond their natural length with instrumental jams (the longest song the band had recorded in their entire career previously had been four minutes ten seconds long, but on this album there are four songs that are longer than that, with *Australia* being nearly seven minutes long.)

However, this is still a truly great album, and it's all the more astonishing then that it did so poorly with the listening public. Not only did the album fail to chart, but of the three singles released from it the first two didn't chart at all and the third only reached number 33. For a band that only recently had had an unbroken run of eight top ten singles to do so poorly suggests that something, somewhere, was very, very wrong.

It could have been very different – *Arthur* was conceived as a series of songs for a Granada TV special, co-written by

Ray Davies and the playwright Julian Mitchell, which would have looked at the history of Britain in the twentieth century through the life of a character, Arthur Morgan, based loosely on Arthur Anning, Davies' brother-in-law.

Unfortunately for the Kinks, the TV show was cancelled fairly close to production, and the Who released their own concept album, also named after its central character, *Tommy*, while the Kinks were still finishing recording. This was partly because there was still a general lack of focus around the band at the time, with several projects in various states of completion – while recording and writing *Arthur* and writing the TV show, Ray Davies was also producing *Turtle Soup*[13] in the USA, while the band were also recording a Dave Davies 'solo' album (which would remain unreleased, although versions of it have appeared on archival releases) and the band were also getting used to new bass player John Dalton.

The recordings with the Turtles, however, had a longer-term impact – while in LA, Davies negotiated an end to the ban on the Kinks performing in the US that the US musicians' union had brought in in 1965. As the band's career in the UK ground to a halt, they were slowly able to build themselves a new career in the US.

The Album

Victoria

Writer: Ray Davies

Lead Vocalist: Ray Davies

---

[13] An absolutely astonishing album by US pop group the Turtles, which manages to combine their witty LA pop sensibility with the gentle wistfulness of *Village Green Preservation Society*. Anyone who likes the Kinks' music must listen to it.

The opening track, and third single from the album, this reached number thirty-three. Lyrically, it's a return to the themes of *Village Green Preservation Society*, but less conflicted – it seems a fairly straightforward paean to the glories of Empire and to Queen Victoria, with only the lines "for this land I shall die" and "the rich were so mean" hinting at the darker themes to come. The lyrics even specifically mention "croquet lawns, village greens".

Musically, however, it's as different from *Village Green* as the Kinks ever got – thudding, heavy, riff-driven rock, extremely bass-heavy and hitting one like a punch in the gut rather than being light, elegant and intellectual. Which is not to say there's no subtlety here – the horn arrangement on the middle eight, in particular, is very well done – but this is the Kinks becoming a rock band, as opposed to a pop group.

The concept of 'rock' as opposed to 'pop' only really started to be seen as a distinction worth making in the late 60s, when most of the bands who wanted to be seen as 'serious artists' started concentrating on albums, making records more heavily influenced by the blues, and turning up their amplification. The Kinks were one of a number of wonderful bands who got left behind (albeit temporarily) by this change – perceived by the hippies as a pop group, while being seen as past it by the younger-skewing singles-buying audience, they could create wonderful records like this and be more or less ignored by both groups of listeners.

Victoria is, though, one of the Kinks' more well-loved singles in retrospect, having been covered by bands as diverse as the Fall and the Kooks over the years.

This is also the first Kinks song to be more listenable in stereo than in mono. The mono mix of this (and of much of the album) is oppressive and bass-heavy. The stereo mix is lighter, more open, and has overall a better balance of instruments.

Yes Sir, No Sir

Writer: Ray Davies

Lead Vocalist: Ray Davies

This track is one of the most extraordinary things in the Kinks' catalogue, a mini-suite in which Davies takes on a number of characters in order to express his anger at authority, using World War I as an excuse.

To the extent Davies' songwriting has any coherent politics at all, it is against all forms of authority and conformity and for the individual, and here he lets that out in a way that he's never previously been able to. He was almost certainly inspired here by the film *Oh! What A Lovely War*, which came out during the early stages of planning of the album, and which combined music-hall songs with a depiction of the horror of World War I.

While World War I had always been controversial, its role in the national myth of Britain had until fairly recently been that of 'The Great War', a war that the country could be proud of. However, as the 60s drew on, and as feeling against war in general was on the increase, the consensus changed to the one that now dominates discussion of the subject – the 'lions led by donkeys' who sacrificed themselves for no good reason. Even the *Doctor Who* story broadcast at the time *Arthur* was being recorded took this line, so common had that view become[14].

Yes Sir, No Sir conveys that sense all too well. It starts with a simple military bass and snare-drum pattern, and a simple four-chord guitar part, over which Davies sings as an infantryman asking for "permission to speak" and "permission to breathe".

---

[14] And I am indebted to Gavin Burrows and Gavin Robinson, in the discussions for a blog post I wrote about that *Doctor Who* story, at http://mindlessones.com/2012/02/11/doctor-who-fifty-stories-for-fifty-years-1969/, for the slightly more nuanced view of that consensus I present here.

We then get the addition of a horn section, and a return of the old favourite technique of holding a chord while the bassline plays a descending scale, as an officer tells the soldier "you're outside and there ain't no admission to our play", and in a parody of the popular World War I song, to "pack up your ambition in your old kit bag/And you'll be happy with a packet of fags".

We then get to the chilling heart of the song, when Davies takes on the persona of an aristocrat, concerned more with maintaining authority than anything else. The last few lines of this section – "Give the scum a gun and make the buggers fight/Just be sure to have deserters shot on sight/If he dies we'll send a medal to his wife", followed by a braying laugh – are among the best things Davies has ever done.

We then return to the trooper for one last verse before...

Some Mother's Son

Writer: Ray Davies

Lead Vocalist: Ray Davies

Easily the best album track the band ever did, this exquisite little ballad uses many of the techniques from *Village Green Preservation Society*, both musical (harpsichord arpeggios, played by Ray Davies, who *did* provide all the keyboard parts on this album, and descending scales) and lyrical (the motif of the photograph again) to totally different effect – the nostalgia here is a mother's memory of her son, shot in the war.

While this song gets much of its power from its generality – the details of the soldier are deliberately kept vague, he's an Unknown Soldier figure rather than a person with a sketched out life history – the real key line here is the seemingly unbearably callous, but simultaneously heartbreaking, line about the mother framing his picture on the wall, "but all dead soldiers look the same". Like so many of Davies' best lines, this has many, many possible interpretations – the way the military makes people conform, the way photographs are framed to look the same way for everyone, but the most touching reading of the line, I think, is the implication that the soldiers killed in the war were not yet fully formed. Boys of eighteen and nineteen for the most part, they hadn't yet had time to develop as distinct individuals, before that opportunity was denied them – which is why it's possible to sing about them so generally.

A heartbreaking song on its own, when listened to in context after *Yes Sir, No Sir* this becomes one of the most effective anti-war songs ever written.

Drivin'

Writer: Ray Davies

Lead Vocalist: Ray Davies

This was the lead-off single from the album, and the first Kinks single not to get into the Top 40 since 1964. In retrospect, it was an insane choice, as it's one of the very weakest songs on the album. It's not bad, just rather substance-free.

Even on here, though, there's still some bite – while it sounds like a purely escapist piece of fluff, the lyrics show why escapism was needed, in the between-wars time in which this is set, "seems like all the world is fighting/they're even talking of a war", and when the characters go for a drive and picnic they'll be followed by debt collectors and rent collectors.

Brainwashed

Writer: Ray Davies

Lead Vocalist: Ray Davies

Another of the weaker songs on the album, this is one of those songs where Davies' vaguely libertarian politics take a fairly nasty turn, and his individualism becomes a contempt for anyone who lives a normal life, with lines like "Look like a real human being but you don't have a mind of your own".

In particular, Davies here blames the "bureaucrats" who give the character to whom he's singing "social security/tax saving benefits" for brainwashing people – a typical libertarian critique of the state, and one which has some validity, but a critique that it's much, much easier to make when, like Davies, you've grown up with those safety nets and also managed to become very wealthy.

Which wouldn't be so bad in itself – there is nothing that says that pop music should be politically 'progressive' (whatever that word actually means) and a critique of social democracy from a right-libertarian perspective, at a time when the revolutionary rhetoric of much of the New Left was starting to fall apart, would be a fair idea for a song, even if I'd disagree with that critique, but here Davies is talking to someone who is a victim of this supposed brainwashing, but seeing that victimhood as a moral failing in the victim.

This kind of arrogant right-libertarian victim-blaming is something we also see a lot of in the works of Frank Zappa, whose attitudes are closer to those of Davies than most critics acknowledge, but except at his early 80s nadir Zappa never wrote anything as musically dull as this.

Australia

Writer: Ray Davies

Lead Vocalist: Ray Davies

A much better song finishes the first side of the album. In the late 50s and early 60s there was a mass wave of emigration from the UK to Australia, which at the time was advertising widely for (white) Commonwealth immigrants, as opposed to its extremely restrictive immigration laws today, and the Davies' sister Rose, and her husband Arthur, had moved over there.

Davies here outlines a dream of a mythical utopian Australia much like the California of the Beach Boys (who he references on the line "we'll surf like they do in the USA", with some very competent Wilsonesque falsetto in the backing), an open, free society very different from the closed, decaying Britain still in thrall to the memory of Queen Victoria, and would have made for a great single.

However, they then choose to spoil the track somewhat (though it's still, on balance, an enjoyable record) by adding onto the three-minute actual song a near four-minute instrumental jam which has little to recommend it (other than the humorous touch of playing the wobble-board, an instrument invented by Australian TV personality and singer Rolf Harris, which would conjure up images of Australia instantly to anyone in the UK, even though it was invented and popularised over here.)

I sometimes sound rather harsher on these freeform instrumental outros than I perhaps should – they are very much an aspect of the time when they were recorded, when the discipline of the three minute pop song was being deprecated in favour of the ability to stretch out and extend songs – but the looser and less disciplined the Kinks' music got, in general, the less successful it seems in retrospect. A band who were recently singing the praises of timeless traditions were now attempting to follow the herd, and it's precisely those points where they do that that the music is at its least successful.

Shangri-La

Writer: Ray Davies

THE ALBUM   121

Lead Vocalist: Ray Davies

This, on the other hand, earns every second of its five minutes and twenty seven seconds. This portrait of a retired (or close to retirement) middle-class suburbanite living in a small house[15] is a far more sympathetic look at the life of the kind of person Davies criticised in *Brainwashed*.

The song starts with two verses based on picking around an Am chord on an acoustic guitar, which would nowadays conjure up *Stairway To Heaven* for most people, but this came out first by several years. With a gentle brass backing coming in in the second verse, we have a description of the protagonist's (presumably Arthur's) contentment in his own little kingdom, with undreamed-of luxuries like a car and indoor toilets. It's gentle, and understanding, and quite lovely.

We then have a few bars in D, with a I-Imaj7-I7 change (a very common way of implying stasis and movement simultaneously in music, used in for example the first line of the Beatles' *Something*), before the song goes into another of Davies' descending scalar bassline sections, but here a harpsichord has come in, and this suits the baroque feeling very well. All of this gives a feeling of movement while staying in almost exactly the same place, which fits the lyric perfectly.

This section's lyric manages the wonderful trick of simultaneously evoking a feeling of security and of being trapped

---

[15] Note for Americans – many houses in the UK are known by names, rather than numbers, and Shangri-La would be a typical example of such a name (the cliched example would be Dunroamin.) Merely stating that a house is named this would, for a British person, mean they would be willing to give near-certain odds that the owners are over 55, have a doorbell that plays a snatch of a sentimental tune, a sticker in their window saying "no cold callers", some form of garden gnome, quite possibly holding a sign saying "gran lives here", and own a small dog, probably a terrier of some kind. The point being that this is a detail which implies a great deal to Davies' intended audience. The song would be very different were the house named "Spunker's Squalor" like the house Mick Avory and Dave Davies had shared a couple of years previously.

– the protagonist has "reached the top and just can't get any higher", "you're in your place and you know who you are", and most damningly "you need not worry, you need not care/You can't go anywhere". The protagonist here is in the same situation as the singer in *Autumn Almanac*, living exactly the life he's chosen, in exactly the place he wants to be, but trapped by that very perfection – he knows that any change he makes to his life would make it worse, so he *can't* change it.

We then have a description of the protagonist's earlier, working life with "a mortgage hanging over his head, but he's too scared to complain, 'cause he's conditioned that way" – the protagonist gets rid of these financial insecurities, he pays off his debts, but he still lives in a state of insecurity.

In the next, rockier, section – almost all built on one chord, again with a descending bass to disguise the fundamentally stationary nature, he's "Too scared to think about how insecure you are" precisely *because* of the security he's in now – having lived a poorer life he knows how fragile it is. Meanwhile, "all the houses on the street all look the same", and the protagonist is suffering an almost schizoid detachment – when the neighbours visit "they say their lines, they drink their tea and then they go", like actors in a play or film rather than real people.

After this, the reprise of the earlier "sit back in your old rocking chair" section, with its brass band backing, sounds absolutely triumphal, the Dm of the rocky section resolving into D major, and the middle-aged man sat in his chair is a figure who has overcome real difficulty to get this eggshell-fragile comfort, and can justly be proud of it.

Shangri-La is one of the best things the Kinks ever recorded, and in the way it uses its epic length to take the listener on an emotional journey it deserves comparison with *A Day In The Life* by the Beatles, *Surf's Up* by the Beach Boys and (the closest resemblance musically) *You Set The Scene* by Love. For all that parts of this album are bloated compared to the band's earlier work, this track shows what they could do with the longer song lengths that were now being allowed.

The only problem with this is that it was released as a single, when it's an utterly unsuitable choice. It's an absolute masterpiece, but it sank without trace, becoming the band's second single in a row not even to make the top forty.

Mr. Churchill Said

Writer: Ray Davies

Lead Vocalist: Ray Davies

This is one of the lesser songs on the album, but a necessary breather after the intensity of *Shangri-La*. A fairly simple song, this just lists pretty much every cliche about the "Blitz spirit" that was (and still is) the principal way the Second World War is viewed in British culture. In the context of the album, a slight satiric edge might be perceived here – everything is portrayed in terms of speeches from Churchill, or Mountbatten, or editorials from Beaverbrook, all of them the kind of authority figure that the rest of the album spends so much time attacking – but I think the song is fundamentally sincere.

She's Bought A Hat Like Princess Marina

Writer: Ray Davies

Lead Vocalist: Ray Davies

One of the most effective songs on the album, this is a look at a particular type of respectable poverty, where people will go hungry in order to keep up the appearance of respectable middle-class living. Both the characters in the song have bought hats that resemble those of the ultra-rich upper-classes – Princess Marina was the Queen's aunt and a member of the royal families of two countries, while Anthony Eden (later the Earl of Avon) was Prime Minister in the 1950s.

The song is presumably set in the mid-1930s, when Britain was still suffering the effects of the Depression, but when Eden was a dashing young politician who was so popular for his looks and fashion sense that Homburg hats were renamed in his honour and he was known as one of "the glamour boys", while Marina had only recently married into the British Royal Family.

We get two verses played relatively straight, over a harpsichord backing, with the pathos of the situation mostly left implicit, before everything breaks down in the middle eight, and the previously tight-laced singer starts bellowing "buddy can you spare me a dime?", referencing the popular Depression-era protest song, before the last verse is done almost in the style of the Bonzo Dog Band, uptempo in a mock-Dixieland style with out-of-tune horns and banjo.

Young And Innocent Days

Writer: Ray Davies

Lead Vocalist: Ray Davies

A rather lovely waltz-time baroque pastiche, once again based around a descending scalar bassline, from the perspective of someone looking back at better times both for the singer and for his lover. One of Davies' best melodies, the lyric is merely serviceable, leading to a song which manages to be unmemorable when one is not listening to it, but enrapturing when it's playing. The instrumental middle eight is particularly beautiful.

Nothing To Say

Writer: Ray Davies

Lead Vocalist: Ray Davies

A filler track in the context of the album, though one suspects it would have been a powerful moment in the TV show, here one of Arthur's children, grown with kids of his own, tells the old man that he won't be spending any more time with him and it's best they go their separate ways (presumably the son is the one who will emigrate to Australia), because while he's fond of the memories of his childhood, the two of them have nothing in common any more.

It's a good and interesting subject for a song, but the musical material doesn't really live up to the topic, just being a straightforward three-chord rocker. It's certainly not a bad track, but nor is it up to the standards of the best material on the album.

Arthur

Writer: Ray Davies

Lead Vocalist: Dave and Ray Davies

And we finish with a country-rock song that points the way to the sound the band would go for on *Muswell Hillbillies*, that tells the whole story of Arthur's life, allowing us to put the rest of the songs into their proper context. And happily, for an album that at times has shown a callous indifference to Arthur and his middle-class conformist type, here the band sing "Arthur, could be that the world was wrong... Arthur, could be you were right all along" before ending on a unison chorus of "Oh we love you and want to help you/Somebody loves you don't you know it?"

By ending on this note, and with a song that ties together the previously disparate songs into some sort of coherent narrative, the band manage to make the album better than the sum of its parts. While it has songs which contain misjudgements, either musically or lyrically, the album as a whole, and in its closing statement, is fundamentally on the side of decency and empathy. There might be an element of contempt in their attitude to Arthur at times (as no doubt there always is when those in their twenties consider those two generations older) but this is still the same band who gave us *Village Green Preservation Society*, a band that can see something noble in the tiny triumphs and failures that make up a normal life. It's not glamorous – not the story of an extraordinary character, there are no pinball wizards or acid queens here – but it's an honest attempt at depicting ordinary life with sympathy and good humour, and as such *Arthur* is almost certainly the best concept album ever recorded.

Bonus Tracks

Plastic Man

Writer: Ray Davies

Lead Vocalist: Ray Davies

The last track that Pete Quaife, the original bass player for the band, ever played on before his acrimonious departure first from the Kinks and shortly thereafter from the music business altogether, was this, the single that almost destroyed the band's career.

It's sad that this was Quaife's swansong, as he deserved better than this. This is Davies attempting, and failing, to write a Kinks song – specifically a song from their commercial high-point a couple of years earlier. Musically, it's fine – a competent enough pastiche of their sound ca. *Dedicated Follower Of Fashion* – if unmemorable, but lyrically it's horrible. An attempt at the earlier satirical style Davies had used in songs like *Well-Respected Man*, it is aimed not at any real person, but at the kind of fantasy of what a conformist middle-class person might be like that an arrogant eighteen-year-old might come up with. It shows no sympathy for the character, and dehumanises him so completely that the song detaches from all reference to reality and becomes about nothing at all.

The attempt at getting more commercial backfired, as it was banned from the radio for using the word "bum", and so only scraped to number 31. The next two singles (*Drivin'* and *Shangri-La*) didn't chart at all. The Kinks would have the very occasional hit single from this point on, but their golden touch for singles success departed with Quaife.

This Man He Weeps Tonight

Writer: Dave Davies

Lead Vocalist: Dave Davies

The B-side for *Shangri-La*, and one of several tracks recorded around the time of *Arthur* for Dave Davies' unreleased solo album *A Hole In The Sock Of*, this Byrds-like jangly folk-rock record would probably have been a better choice for the A-side. Despite not being as good a song as its A-side, this is undoubtedly the more commercial song — it's a straightforward verse/chorus song with a catchy riff and good harmonies, while still having an up-to-date heavy rock sound.

Lyrically, it's a simple song about the break-up of a relationship and regret for plans made that will never now be put into action. The most interesting line is "I thought our thing would last, 'cause it said so in my horoscope", which is the first indication in any of his songs of Dave Davies' interest in astrology, which would soon broaden to include occultism and the 'magick' of the Golden Dawn, and be the most important influence on him for most of his life.

Mindless Child Of Motherhood

Writer: Dave Davies

Lead Vocalist: Dave Davies

Another Dave Davies solo track, this time the B-side to *Drivin'*, this is almost painful to listen to because of the sheer weight of emotion behind it. A howl of pain about the end of his teenage relationship and the child he had never seen, this has none of the ambiguity or metaphor of the earlier songs he had written, instead containing lines like "I know that it's unfair to bear a bastard son, but why do you hide, babe, when we could have shared a love?"

The song's construction is extraordinary, barely staying in the same time signature for two bars straight, and having a chorus that alternates bars of sixes and sevens, while following perfectly the emotional logic of the confused, disoriented lyric. This would definitely *not* have made a good single, but is the best thing Dave Davies had written to this point.

Creeping Jean

Writer: Dave Davies

Lead Vocalist: Dave Davies

The B-side to Dave Davies' solo single *Hold My Hand*, this has almost exactly the same melody as Ray's earlier *Rainy Day In June*. Lyrically, it's a rather nasty, misogynist rant against a girlfriend leaving him, but musically it's a powerful band performance. Just a shame they'd already recorded the tune with better lyrics.

Lincoln County

Writer: Dave Davies

Lead Vocalist: Dave Davies

A 1968 solo Dave Davies single (and thus featuring Pete Quaife on bass), this is very unusual for Dave Davies, as it sounds musically for all the world like a Ray Davies song, descending bassline, harpsichord and all. While it's a little harder in tone than most of the *Village Green Preservation Society* material, it's no more so than *Last Of The Steam-Powered Trains* and with its theme of returning home it would have fit the earlier album nicely.

Lyrically, it's less strong – it's a coming home from jail song built up out of cliches from country songs, and doesn't seem to have been written with any real conviction – but musically it's one of Dave Davies' best songs from this time. Unfortunately it didn't chart.

Hold My Hand

Writer: Dave Davies

Lead Vocalist: Dave Davies

Another non-charting single by Dave Davies, again featuring Quaife on bass rather than Dalton, this one is an obvious attempt at sounding like Bob Dylan, right down to impersonating Dylan's voice (it actually comes spookily close to the sound Dylan was getting on the *Nashville Skyline* album, which was being recorded when this was released.) Even more than that, though, it sounds like the ramshackle boozy soul-folk that Rod Stewart (a former schoolmate of the Davies brothers and Quaife) would come out with towards the end of the year.

It's an odd choice for a single, having odd time signatures in the chorus, which breaks down as far as I can tell into two bars of seven, two of four, one of six and one of four, though it could be written in a variety of other ways – the pulses are all over the place. The chorus also, with its seven-beat bars and "three blind mice" melody bears a very slight resemblance to a countrified version of *All You Need Is Love*.

Not Davies' best work, it was a brave song to go with as a single, and deserved to do better than it did.

Mr Shoemaker's Daughter

Writer: Dave Davies

Lead Vocalist: Dave Davies

A perfectly pleasant, but derivative track that seems to have been built up out of bits of Ray Davies' songs *Mr Reporter* and *Mr Pleasant*, along with a brief statement of the riff from the Searchers' *Needles And Pins* by a horn section, the lyrics to this are the kind of fluff that would have been a minor hit for Herman's Hermits four or five years earlier. This was intended for Dave Davies' solo album, but remained unreleased until a 1980s Japanese-only compilation of Dave Davies solo tracks.

Lola versus Powerman And The Moneygoround, Part One

Lola Versus Powerman And The Moneygoround, Part One is a difficult album to assess from this distance. Artistically, it's a clear step down from *Arthur*, but at the same time it sparked a short-lived commercial resurgence for the band, at least in the singles chart, providing the Kinks with their last two UK top ten singles in *Lola* and *Apeman*.

Musically, the album is as inventive as ever, if in a heavier rock style than the band had had prior to *Arthur*, but lyrically the album is somewhat lacking, being self-obsessed in a way that the earlier albums hadn't been. Fully half the songs are about how hard it is being a rock star and how managers, record companies, publishing companies and the rest of the music business are all out to make pop singers' lives as difficult as possible.

Of course, for those of us who aren't rock stars, this may seem a little hard to relate to – it's hard to feel much sympathy for someone who is still, in the grand scheme of things, being paid vast sums of money for doing a job that is far more enjoyable than most people could dream of.

However, while it may be hard to sympathise, Ray Davies had a real reason to be angry. A contractual dispute with Eddie

Kassner, his publisher, dating back to 1965 had meant that for the previous five years – the Kinks' prime earning period – he had not received a penny of the songwriting royalties he was due. He'd eventually settled out of court in order to get any of the money at all, agreeing to a lower royalty rate and paying Kassner £30,000 (the equivalent of £653,000 in 2012 money) so he could get some of what he was owed. One can perhaps understand his frustration.

Lola vs Powerman is a transitional album for the Kinks in a number of ways. It was their last proper studio album for Pye records, the label they'd been with from the start of their career – they recorded the largely-instrumental soundtrack to the film *Percy* and then left for RCA Records. It's also the first album to feature new keyboard player John "Baptist" Gosling, and is a clear step toward the blend of country music and heavy rock the band would achieve on their last truly great album, *Muswell Hillbillies*, though it's not quite there yet. However, the songwriting is tighter than it was on *Arthur,* with almost all the songs coming in under four minutes, and almost half being under three. When a song begins to pall, another one will be along soon, and there's still a better than average chance it'll be a good one.

In this piece I will have to deal slightly more with the personal lives of the band members than I like to, simply because the songs themselves are so personal.

The Album

The Contenders

Writer: Ray Davies

Lead Vocalist: Ray Davies

This track starts with a lovely little two-chord bluegrass harmony section, Ray and Dave Davies harmonising with each other over a dobro and banjo backing, sounding almost like the 'rebel country' music made by people like Steve Earle a few decades later, before crashing into a Canned Heat style harmonica-led boogie (and a key change from E to A), with some of the best harmonica playing on a Kinks record.

Lyrically, this seems to be in equal parts about Davies' wish to escape from domesticity (his first marriage was rapidly heading towards collapse at this point) and about his ambitions for the band – he doesn't want to be a manual worker or to go into a respectable job, but he's "got to get out of this life somehow". When he sings "We're not the greatest when when we're separated/But when we're together I think we're going to make it", he could be singing to the "little mammy" of the first line (presumably his first wife, Rasa), but equally he sounds like he's singing to his brother and the rest of his bandmates.

Strangers

Writer: Dave Davies

Lead Vocalist: Dave Davies

So it's appropriate that the next song (which is segued into – the album is sequenced almost without gaps between the songs) would be this outstretched hand from Dave Davies to his brother.

The first song that Dave Davies had had on an album since *Something Else*, this may be the best song he ever wrote. Around the time that *Lola Vs Powerman* was being recorded, Dave Davies had had a mental breakdown, but communication between the brothers had got so bad (and Ray Davies was under so much pressure himself) that Ray had not even been aware of this. However, Dave had managed to pull himself back from the brink with a variety of New Age beliefs, and now saw himself at the beginning of a new spiritual journey.

The song recognises that Dave Davies is starting from a place where all his previous certainties have been shattered, but that he can see a way forward – and that while his brother can't see that way forward, he knows that he's been in a similar situation, and wants to offer him help. He recognises that the two are drifting apart, but there's a deeper bond between them.

With Dave Davies' trademark metrical irregularity, but with a very simple backing track (two acoustic guitars, piano, organ, and what sounds like just a kick drum and floor tom), this is a wonderfully tender, touching song of brotherly love, and the best thing on the album.

Denmark Street

Writer: Ray Davies

Lead Vocalist: Ray Davies

A rather slight song about the music publishing industry (Denmark Street was the street in London where almost all the UK's music publishers were based), this combines pub-singalong piano, country-rock and 1940s pop (one section sounds very like George Formby) into a style which prefigures quite a lot of the pub rock sound of the late 70s. Were this song slightly more funky, it could fit musically quite comfortably with the work of Ian Dury and The Blockheads.

Lyrically, however, it's a nothing piece of fluff, just saying that music publishers don't necessarily like the music they publish.

Get Back In The Line

Writer: Ray Davies

Lead Vocalist: Ray Davies

THE ALBUM 135

This is possibly the hardest song on this album to judge from the perspective of the twenty-first century, because it's a very political song, but talking about something that no longer exists.

In the 1970s, unions were far more powerful in the UK than they are today. Between the decline of Britain's manufacturing and mining industries, legislation brought in by the Thatcher and Major governments, and European law banning 'closed shops', unions in Britain today have little power and relatively low membership. In the 1970s, however, they were a major political force, and there was a growing consensus that they were using that power harmfully.

This consensus (which is the accepted view on nearly every side today) may or may not have been correct (I have relatives who were trade union officials at the time whose stories of some of the more prominent *causes celebres* of the time differ wildly from the accepted view), but that was certainly the belief among an increasing proportion of society at the time, and that clearly included Ray Davies.

So in this ballad, one of the best melodies he wrote on the album, he writes from the point of view of a working man trying to earn a living and being blocked by "the union man".

It may seem that this song, about British working-class life, has no place on an album which is mostly about the music business, but Ray Davies had had his own problems with unions. From 1965 through 1969 – the band's prime years as a singles band in the UK – they had been banned from playing in the USA as a result of a dispute with the American Federation of Musicians, a dispute which had led to their career crashing into obscurity over there.

Davies clearly (and understandably) thought that the frustrations he experienced from the Musicians' Union were much of a piece with the problems he was having with his managers, publishers and record company, and so felt a great deal of sympathy with those who were in the power of the unions in the

UK.

Musically, this is the clearest example for a while of how Ray Davies' love of descending scalar basslines is clearly influenced by Bach. Here the organ part gives the song something of the flavour of organ works like *Liebster Jesu, wir sind hier* or *O Lamm Gottes, unschuldig,* though the melody is all Davies' own. The bassline is more cleverly worked out than some of the earlier stepwise basslines have been, though – while in the chorus it's mostly based around a descending scale in G, when the chord gets to Em, the bassline suddenly starts rising, getting to A – a tone higher than it started – before dropping back to D, which would have been the natural next note in the descent after Em, and continuing to go down.

This sudden rise to higher than the bassline has been previously, followed by a precipitous drop to lower than it was before, melds beautifully with the lyrics – the rise from E to A starts on the phrase "the sun begins to shine", before the drop down and descent on the line "Then he walks right past and I know that I've got to get back in the line". Rarely has Davies ever matched musical form with lyrical content to such devastating effect.

Lola

Writer: Ray Davies

Lead Vocalist: Ray Davies

The Kinks' biggest hit for many years – their first UK top ten hit for three years and their first in the US since *Well-Respected Man* – was this track about meeting a trans person in a bar, and going back to have sex with her unaware she's trans – and then not minding too much when he finds out.

I've dreaded writing about this song, because it's witty, clever, and one of the catchiest things Ray Davies ever wrote, but it also perpetuates some negative stereotypes about trans people. However, it *also* shows more respect to trans people than any other pop song I could think of, so I decided to ask some of my trans friends what they thought of the song. The poet Rachel Zall responded:

> Well, speaking for myself as a trans woman:
>
> Certainly it's hard to argue that it doesn't repeat and reinforce all sorts of tired transmisogynist tropes, or that the song doesn't have a nasty hetero-cis sneer underneath it.
>
> But for lots of folks, as you said, it was at least a mention that we exist that was framed in a non-hostile way, and for folks who've never heard themselves represented before, a song suggesting that one might at least be lovable to someone somewhere, even ironically, can mean a lot. (I mean, four decades later, can you name another love song to a trans woman? I can't.)
>
> Personally, for just that reason it meant a lot to me when I was a kid (along with "Walk On The Wild Side" and Rachel Pollack's run on *Doom Patrol*), so I'm always a bit kinder to it than I can justify.
>
> Having said all that, I think this speaks more to the desperation many trans women feel trying to find any even theoretically positive depiction of ourselves in popular culture. Divorced from the culture around it, the song is hugely problematic and hard to defend, but in context, it seems better than it is by virtue of being a small, sickly fish in an otherwise empty pond. Which is kinda sad, actually.

Which is about what I thought the reaction would be – the song is problematic now, even though at the time it was a fairly progressive song.

(And incidentally, no, I can't think of any other songs about being attracted to a trans woman, off the top of my head – other than, actually, the Kinks' later song *Out Of The Wardrobe*, which manages to urge tolerance for trans people while simultaneously being rather homophobic.)

Lola was actually based on several real experiences the band and people around them had. Most of the Kinks were not entirely heterosexual, and Mick Avory apparently spent a lot of time in trans nightclubs. At various times, Ray Davies has said the song is about Avory, about his own (apparently non-sexual) meeting with Candy Darling, and about the Kinks' manager Robert Wace going home with a trans woman, too drunk to care.

Oddly, the biggest problem this song had with getting radio play was not the subject matter, nor the ending of the song (with its implication of our protagonist performing fellatio on Lola), but the mention of "Coca Cola" in the lyric – the BBC were then not allowed to mention brand names, and Davies had to make a 6000-mile round trip to overdub the word "cherry" over "Coca" for the single release, in order to get it played. Both versions of the song are on the current release of the album.

Dave Davies has often claimed that he wrote the music for this song, uncredited. Whatever the correct credits, this is one of the best singles the Kinks ever released, and has now entered the popular culture to such an extent that this was the song chosen for Ray Davies to play when he performed at the Queen's Jubilee concert in 2002.

Top Of The Pops

Writer: Ray Davies

Lead Vocalist: Ray Davies

A tedious heavy riffer with no real reason to exist, this is just a song about how having a hit single makes you popular, a sentiment that very few of the listeners will be able to appreciate.

The two main points of interest here are the line "I've been invited to a dinner with a prominent queen", presumably included so that *Lola* would fit in with the rest of the album (other than that line there are no connections between the subject of *Lola* and the music-business stresses of the rest of the album), and the last line, in which Davies puts on an 'hilarious' mock-Jewish voice to play an agent.

One of the more positive changes over the last forty years in the UK is that outright mockery of ethnic minorities is no longer considered acceptable in polite company, but in the early 1970s – and even into the mid-80s – there was considered nothing wrong with even fairly small-l liberal comedians blacking up or making fun of Jewish people. In that context, Davies' 'comedy' voice at the end of this song was perfectly acceptable – he's doing a caricature of the stereotypical showbiz agent, not dissimilar to those done by people like Monty Python or The Goodies. Today, it mars the album, and comes across as very unpleasant.

Oddly, this was used as the opening music for the tenth anniversary special edition of *Top Of The Pops* itself.

The Moneygoround

Writer: Ray Davies

Lead Vocalist: Ray Davies

The best of the music-business songs on the album by a long way, this is a short (one minute forty-three) romp, in the style of Noel Coward or Flanders And Swann, through the details of the contracts that Davies was enmeshed in. While it's obviously biased towards Davies (Robert Wace and Grenville Collins, both of whom are named in the lyric, have objected to the line "do they all deserve/money from a song that they've never heard?", claiming that they knew and loved the music of the band when they were managing them), the description is one that anyone who knows about the music industry at that time will recognise as being largely accurate, with layers of publishers and managers all taking a cut before the artist gets a penny.

Musically, this is a pre-war show tune, from the almost-ragtime verses (with yet another Davies descending bassline) to the melodramatic bridge (Davies sounding wonderfully hammy on "I thought they were my friends", his tongue firmly in cheek even as the point of the song is serious) and the bouncy chorus, with its lyrical quote from *The Music Goes Round And Round*. *The Moneygoround* also has a slight musical resemblance to that song, a hit for the Tommy Dorsey band in 1936 that was a pop standard when Davies was growing up. The resemblance to *The Music Goes Round And Round* can be heard most closely in Russ Conway's piano version, though I don't recommend anyone listen to that track.

This, however, is a delight. Funny, clever, and entertaining, and complaining about a real problem without being angsty.

This Time Tomorrow

Writer: Ray Davies

Lead Vocalist: Ray Davies

Side two opens with this, one of the most affecting tracks on the album, even though like many of the better tracks on this album it admits of less analysis than some of the more complex music on the band's mid-sixties records.

Staying almost entirely in the key of G (apart from an occasional B major chord, usually just as a passing chord), this is a curiously melancholy upbeat song about a long plane journey home, to "fields full of houses". The most interesting feature in the track, and the one that lifts it into the top tier of the band's early-70s work, is the way the banjo part (played by Dave Davies, with a very unusual attack – he's playing it like a guitar player, rather than a banjo player), with its fast-picked arpeggios, is doubled by Gosling's piano. The odd, skipping, rippling effect created by having two such different instruments play such a fast arpeggiated part on an otherwise mid-tempo song is one that must have been hellish to achieve in the studio, but which paid off, making this track endlessly listenable.

A Long Way From Home

Writer: Ray Davies

Lead Vocalist: Ray Davies

And after the plane touches down, you find "you're still a long way from home". This piano ballad seems to be addressed to both Dave Davies and to Ray himself. For Ray Davies throughout his career, losing touch with one's roots seems to be the single worst thing possible, even as he clearly grows to have less and less in common with the poor North London people he grew up with.

Here he sings about how "your wealth will never make you stronger", because "you don't know me" from the perspective of someone who knew a rich star when he was a "runny-nosed and scruffy kid". Whether this is Ray singing to Dave, or Ray taking on the persona of someone from Muswell Hill talking to Ray, it's fair to say that the critique in the song summed up how both men felt at the time.

The song is very pretty, but curiously forgettable – I have listened to this album hundreds of times, and on the day I wrote this piece I listened to the album five times in a row before I started writing, but I still thought "Which one was that, then?" when I came to write about it. It works in the context of the album, and it clearly meant a lot to the band, but it's not a highlight.

Rats

Writer: Dave Davies

Lead Vocalist: Dave Davies

Musically, Dave Davies' second song on the album is an early heavy metal track that could have been recorded by Deep Purple or Black Sabbath with little change. It's not a genre I particularly like, but it seems a competent enough example of the style, if out of place on this album.

Lyrically, however, this is one of the strongest and strangest things on the record, a hallucinatory scream of despair at the music business people he sees as "rats jumping on and off my back" whose "hate spreads just like infection". It's clearly the work of a troubled man, and is possibly the most unfiltered, honest thing on the whole album. It was the B-side to *Apeman*.

Apeman

Writer: Ray Davies

Lead Vocalist: Ray Davies

The second single from the album, and the band's last top ten hit in the UK, was this calypso song, which returns to Davies' regular themes of wanting to get back to nature and a simpler life, rather than live in a civilised world with "the overpopulation and inflation and starvation and the crazy politicians".

Much like *Top Of The Pops*, this song has been accused of having what gets described euphemistically as "outdated racial attitudes". And in a sense it does – this song is from a time when it was considered reasonable to sing in a comedy fake-Carribean

THE ALBUM

voice, which would probably be considered unacceptable today by most people but was, like the "Jewish" voice in *Top Of The Pops*, considered perfectly normal at the time. The voice is 'outdated', but no worse in that respect than many other products of its times (which is not necessarily to defend those other products.)

The problem comes when the 'outdated' comedy voice is combined with lyrics that contain the line "I'm a King Kong man, I'm a voodoo man, I'm an apeman". The combination of a stereotypically 'black' vocal sound with references to apes and voodoo is at best an unfortunate one, and one that has caused several people to see the song as racist.

However, while I'm not going to argue that there is nothing problematic about the song, I don't believe this song was intended in a racist manner, and I can't imagine that it occurred to Davies for a millisecond that the conjunction of the ape imagery and the voice could be taken to have any racist implications.

Certainly, the *faux*-Carribean feel of the song seems to have been taken by real calypsonians as being a mostly-sincere tribute, rather than an insult – a cover version of this was recorded less than a year later by the Esso Trinidad Steel Band as the opening track of their self-titled album[16].

Certainly, in retrospect, it would have been better had Davies not put on that particular 'funny' voice when singing that particular set of lyrics, but I do think intentions count for a lot, and this isn't the song of someone with bad intentions.

Leaving that to one side, is the song any good?

Well, yes, it is. Other than the piano part at the start (played to sound like a steel band), this is musically almost a straight reworking of *Lola*, with similar instrumentation (including the prominent dobro that's all over the album), feel and

---

[16] This was reissued in 2011 on Bananastan Records, the label of Van Dyke Parks, the album's producer, and is essential listening.

chord sequence. It seems a clear attempt to recapture lightning, having much the same resemblance to *Lola* that *All Day (And All Of The Night)* had to *You Really Got Me*. *Apeman* was so much *Lola* part two that Davies even had to make another transatlantic plane trip to drop in another single word to get the song played on the radio; this time when the BBC weren't sure whether the air pollution was "fogging" or "fucking" up Davies' eyes.

Apeman, however, floats where *Lola* lumbers. Where *Lola* is by far the more instantly impressive track, *Apeman* sticks with the listener, and is an absolutely perfect pop record, and the last truly great Kinks single.

Powerman

Writer: Ray Davies

Lead Vocalist: Ray Davies

A dull, plodding rocker, comparing the "Powerman" who's "got my money and my publishing rights" with Napoleon, Genghis Khan, Hitler and Mussolini. Possibly comparing Edward Kassner (whose parents died in Auschwitz) with Adolf Hitler was not the best way to get people's sympathy. Failing that, Davies could have tried writing a more interesting song to put the comparison in.

Got To Be Free

Writer: Ray Davies

Lead Vocalist: Ray Davies

And we finish the album with a song that ties together its themes, both lyrically (the themes of wanting to escape from the people making Davies a "slave" and live free like "a flea or a proud butterfly"– he even reuses the line about "the bugs and the spiders and flies" from *Apeman*) and musically. In particular it returns to the bluegrass section from the start of *The Contenders* and turns it into a full song.

The verses, which stick closely to the feel of that section of *The Contenders*, work well, with surprisingly authentic-sounding bluegrass banjo and dobro playing. The choruses work a little less well, sounding like an attempt to sound like the Rolling Stones in their more country-blues moments.

The song, like the album it's closing, is something of a curate's egg, veering from dull to surprisingly effective. The best moments of the album are as good as anything the band had done, but even those are problematic in a way earlier work hadn't been, while the worst moments were inferior to anything the band had done since *Face To Face*.

Percy

The Kinks' final album for Pye Records is one that is impossible to listen to in the correct context, because that correct context has never existed. It was written as the soundtrack for the film *Percy*, an alleged comedy about a penis transplant starring Hywel Bennet and Britt Ekland, and so as programmatic music it should be listened to in the context of the film. Except that Ray Davies stormed out of the film's premiere because his music had been so chopped up by the film's makers, so clearly what made it to the film is not what Davies intended.

So the best we can do is to judge the album on its own merits, except that the music was never primarily intended as an album, and so much of the music doesn't really work as a separate listening experience either.

Possibly the best thing for a listener who wants a good musical experience is to listen to just the highlights from the album. The songs *God's Children*, *The Way Love Used To Be*, *Moments* and *Dreams* were released as an EP, and that EP is as good as anything the Kinks were doing around this time. The best of this music is better than the best of *Lola Vs Powerman*, but it's surrounded by instrumental filler.

That said, even the filler is perfectly listenable for the most part – it's just not interesting, either as music or as a stage in the Kinks' artistic development.

For these reasons, this will be the shortest of these essays by some way. It's a shame, though, that Davies didn't get to have his work treated with enough respect that we could hear what it sounded like in its proper context.

The Album

God's Children

Writer: Ray Davies

Lead Vocalist: Ray Davies

Generally considered the highlight of the album, *God's Children* is one of Davies' return-to-nature songs, this time arguing that "we are all God's children" and that "Man...didn't make you and he didn't make me/And he's got no right to turn us into machines."

Musically, this is very Dylanesque, with a simple I-IV-V chorus, and verses that aren't much more complex, and a string section essentially acting as a pad in much the same way Dylan would use a Hammond organ.

It's not a completely thought-out song, but there's an emotional honesty to the track that makes it work.

Lola

Writer: Ray Davies

Lead Vocalist: instrumental

This, on the other hand, really doesn't work at all. A nearly five-minute instrumental version of the band's recent hit, performed in the pseudo-funk style that is stereotypically used in 70s porn films, all chittering hi-hat and mildly distorted guitars, but with the vocal melody stated by a Hammond organ in a way that sounds incongruously like the work of Reggie Dixon.

The Way Love Used To Be

Writer: Ray Davies

Lead Vocalist: Ray Davies

A rather lovely little ballad, this is by far the best thing on the album, and is also far better than anything on *Lola Vs Powerman*. Based around a simple fingerpicked folk-style acoustic guitar part, doubled by piano, but with a string section that has some of the best orchestral arrangements of any Kinks album, dominated by cellos, with a very thin, barely audible, violin line at the top, this is musically simple, beginner stuff, but it's the right kind of simple. This could easily have fit onto Colin Blunstone's *One Year*, which is praise as high as it comes.

Davies' marriage was going through a rough patch at this time, and this song about wanting to get away from the cares of the world and "talk about the way love used to be" is the work of a man who desperately wants to fix what is broken. This is possibly the best Kinks song of the post-60s era, but doesn't really admit of much analysis – it works so well because of its simplicity.

Completely

Writer: Ray Davies

Lead Vocalist: instrumental

A ditchwater-dull blues instrumental based loosely on the melody of *Amazing Grace*, this plods along for three minutes and thirty-nine seconds of nothingness.

Running Around Town

Writer: Ray Davies

Lead Vocalist: instrumental

A nice little fragment, this starts as a rather frenetic, jug-bandish reworking of the melodic theme from *God's Children*, performed on acoustic guitar and harmonica, before easing into a slow, arpeggiated, guitar/piano/harmonica fade.

Moments

Writer: Ray Davies

Lead Vocalist: Ray Davies

Stylistically rather odd, this is a mix between French *chanson* and the kind of 70s divorce rock[17] that one expects to hear sung by a jumpsuited Elvis, occasionally hitting on something that sounds almost like Jake Thackray.

Based around the old Davies trick of the descending scalar bassline, this seems not properly thought out, an emotional expression (a confessional about his failing marriage – "I said I'd never do you wrong but then I go and do the same again/I don't know why") that hasn't been completely fitted into the formal structure of the pop song. Unfortunately, Davies' overly-mannered vocal here distances that emotion enough that the song doesn't quite come off, but it's a brave effort.

Animals In The Zoo

Writer: Ray Davies

Lead Vocalist: Ray Davies

---

[17] A style of music that became briefly popular in the early 1970s, as the first marriages of a lot of the older baby boomers started failing, and musicians of that age started putting out albums of "sensitive" songs apologising to their wives.

A three-chord rocker based loosely on a Bo Diddley beat, but with Davies doing his Carribean accent again, this is another of Davies' songs about needing to get back to nature – "You're locked up but I'm on the loose/But I can't quite tell who's looking at who/Because I'm an animal too". It's the kind of thing you'd write if you wanted to write something that sounded a bit like early 70s Kinks, and is catchy enough, but tellingly wasn't included on the EP of the better material from the album.

Just Friends

Writer: Ray Davies

Lead Vocalist: Ray Davies

One of the strangest, and strongest, things on the album, this shows the growing influence of Kurt Weill on Davies' songwriting – an influence which would come to dominate the *Preservation* album.

Starting with a statement of the melody, played presumably on a celesta, but sounding like a music box, this waltz-time piece then goes into a speak-sung Weimar cabaret style performance, alternating between Davies singing, backed by strings, and a tinkling solo harpsichord answering Davies' phrases.

In this section, Davies sings in a light, pre-war vocal style, with lyrics that show the character he is playing is trying to reassure but is very, very scary – "I shall not molest you, I shan't rape your brain". He then takes on a slightly less sinister persona, this time in a comically vibrato voice reminiscent of Rudy Valee, to repeat the same sentiments over a faster-moving string part.

The track then moves into a baroque instrumental orchestration of the main theme (though perhaps with too simple a string part to have the true baroque feel), led by a harpsichord. The whole thing feels curiously like the work Randy Newman was to do a year or so later, both in the orchestral style and in the use of the unreliable, creepy narrator.

Whip Lady

Writer: Ray Davies

Lead Vocalist: instrumental

Forty seconds of rather interesting minimalist music built up from several layered piano parts playing simple repeating motifs in $\frac{6}{8}$ (with a guitar and bass coming in toward the end), followed by forty seconds of loud rock music with some technically impressive drumming.

Dreams

Writer: Ray Davies

Lead Vocalist: Ray Davies

The most complex song on the album in terms of structure, this is still a comparatively weak song by Davies' standards.

We start with a verse over slow arpeggiated keyboards (based around I and V7 chords with the occasional IV thrown in), doubled with acoustic guitar as on several other tracks around this time. The second verse, following immediately after, is the same melody and chord sequence, but over a sluggish, grinding, rock riff.

There then follows a quick drum fill, leading into a slow ten-bar keyboard solo, based around yet another descending scalar bassline, with a feel that seems to be going for Bach, but is let down by a guitar- and drum-heavy mix.

We then get a seven-bar chorus, with a IV-I chord sequence underpinned by another descending scalar bassline, before suddenly going into an instrumental break consisting of slowly arpeggiated I-IV-V-I chords played by a piano with an organ pad.

We then get a heavy rock version of the verse, a second chorus, another verse, then seven bars of the arpeggios, played at twice the earlier speed, on harpsichord, before the heavy rock style comes in for one final verse and then a repetition of the verse riff to fade.

The song shows some of the ambition of a *Shangri-La* or *Autumn Almanac* in its arrangement and construction, but alas has a paucity of musical ideas, and outstays its welcome.

Helga

Writer: Ray Davies

Lead Vocalist: instrumental

A generically "Mediterranean" instrumental, with wordless vocals from Davies, this features Spanish guitar and what sounds like a bouzouki, playing a $\frac{6}{8}$ melody that owes something to the theme from *Zorba The Greek, El Paso* and to *The Last Waltz*.

Willesden Green

Writer: Ray Davies

Lead Vocalist: John Dalton

This is notable as the only track in the Kinks' entire career to have a lead vocal by a band member other than one of the Davies brothers, as John Dalton performs what seems to be an inept (probably deliberately so) attempt at an Elvis impression.

The song itself is a parody of *Detroit City*, a country song by Bobby Bare that had been a UK top ten hit for Tom Jones in 1967, and has the same melody and, like *Detroit City*, a lyric about missing one's hometown when far away and wanting to get a train back, including a recitative section in the middle.

The joke of the song is that while the singer in *Detroit City* lives in Detroit and misses the cotton fields of the South, the singer in *Willesden Green* has only moved as far as Fulham and Golders Green from his home area of Willesden (all three of these areas are within eleven miles each other, all within London.)

This combination of country music and focusing on a specific area of London would be used more seriously on the band's next album, *Muswell Hillbillies*, but here it's just played for laughs.

God's Children - The End

Writer: Ray Davies

Lead Vocalist: instrumental

Twenty-seven seconds of reprise of the opening track, with the melody played on an acoustic guitar, closes what is the least interesting Kinks album up to this point.

The Early RCA Albums (1971-74)

Muswell Hillbillies

The Kinks' first album for RCA Records is perhaps the last one that can be seen as an unalloyed artistic success. While the Kinks, and Ray and Dave Davies as solo artists, would occasionally produce great work after this point, usually the quality of the work was in inverse proportion to its artistic ambitions. Where Ray Davies came up with long, complex, narrative works, these fell flat, but the band could still create great pop songs as late as the mid-1980s and *Come Dancing*.

Muswell Hillbillies, on the other hand, has a unity of theme and form that makes the album as a whole work better than the individual songs on it. While not a 'concept album' in the sense that many of the band's later works would be, it is an album that has a definite theme, with every aspect of the record subordinate to it.

This is the most political work that Ray Davies ever created, and I have to say upfront that while sympathetic to many of the concerns in the album, it's from a different point-of-view from my own, and that will necessarily come out in my reaction to the record. Davies' argument (insofar as it's a coherent argument rather than a set of contradictory emotional reactions) in this album is that eccentricity and difference are being crushed by an excessively interfering government, and by social planning that destroys communities.

While I can agree with that, my viewpoint is fundamentally liberal, while Davies' argument appears to be a reactionary one

– that all attempts to change people's lives are necessarily for the worst, and that the old ways were always the best. Davies then contrasts the shattered, depressed lives of the British working classes with a rose-tinted view of the USA as filtered through film and TV, implicitly arguing that Britain in the early 1970s had had all its spirit crushed, to the point where even its dreams had to be imported from elsewhere.

For Britons of Davies' generation, America had a totemic power it perhaps lacks today. While Britain went through austerity and rationing in the 1950s, when Davies was a small boy, and much of the landscape had been devastated by bombing during the Second World War, America was experiencing unprecedented prosperity, and this was never more evident than in its cultural exports. From the UK, it was very easy to ignore the horrors of segregation, the pressures to conform, and the growth of what President Eisenhower referred to as "the military-industrial complex", and see a country that was youthful, energetic and growing, while Britain appeared to be in terminal decline.

Musically, the album reflects this with its use of very British versions of American musical idioms. At its base this is a country album, but it's overlaid with trad jazz, courtesy of the latest additions to the band's line-up, The Mike Cotton Sound[18]. Trad jazz is an odd musical form, which had enjoyed a brief flowering of popularity in Britain in the 1950s and early 60s. It was an attempt to slavishly recreate the music of 1920s jazzmen like Sidney Bechet and Bix Beiderbecke, but much like the later British blues bands (many of whom had their roots in trad bands) it grew into something distinct, with only a nodding

---

[18] The Mike Cotton Sound started out as trad jazz group The Mike Cotton Jazzmen in the 1950s, before becoming a beat group and later a soul group in the 1960s (Jim Rodford, the bass player with this line-up, would become the Kinks' bass player from 1978 to 1996.) By this point, though, Cotton had dropped the rhythm section and vocalists from his band, becoming solely a horn section.

similarity to its influences. Musicians like Humphrey Lyttleton, Acker Bilk and Chris Barber had been huge stars in the UK while the Davies brothers were children (and indeed Ray Davies' first paying musical work was as a guitarist in a trad band) and so trad jazz perfectly encapsulated the album's themes – a rather shabby British attempt to imitate the past glories of the US, itself now almost forgotten, but one which nevertheless had a power of its own.

The album also features a chorus of female backing vocalists – and like the Mike Cotton Sound, this would be added to the band for both tours and records over the next few years.

Unfortunately, while this album is much better than *Lola Vs Powerman*, it had no standout singles like *Lola* or *Apeman*, and it essentially marked the end of the Kinks' career as a commercial force in their home country, even as they were slowly getting noticed in the US.

The Album

20th Century Man

Writer: Ray Davies

Lead Vocalist: Ray Davies

The opening track sets out the blatantly reactionary tone of the album most clearly. Over a lumbering acoustic- and slide-guitar riff similar to the music the Rolling Stones were recording at the same time, Davies denounces the twentieth century and the very notion of progress, saying "You keep all your smart modern writers, give me William Shakespeare", attacking the welfare state for "rul[ing] by bureaucracy", and blaming the government for taking away his privacy and liberty.

Now, one's reaction to this song will be almost entirely based on to what extent one agrees with Davies' complaints, and I can sympathise with some of them, especially the concern for individual liberties (and if Davies thought that the early 1970s were a time when civil liberties were being eroded, what must he have made of the ensuing few decades?) but I also think it's far easier to criticise the welfare state if you've lived your entire life with the knowledge that free healthcare and unemployment benefits were available to you if you needed them, than it was for the generation before Davies', who had to fight for these things.

Possibly the line that sums the song up the most is "Whatever happened to the green pleasant fields of Jerusalem?" – Davies agrees with William Blake that industrialisation has a demeaning, degrading effect on people, but where Blake's poem was a revolutionary call to arms – "I will not cease from mental fight/Nor shall my sword sleep in my hand/Til we have built Jerusalem/In England's green and pleasant land" – Davies' song is more of a *Daily Mail* leader.

However, we must not necessarily assume that this song represents Davies' views exactly – the first few songs on the album, at least, seem to be connected and in character, sung by someone who, like the Mr Pilgrim of Lewis' essay, is driven mad by a compulsory purchase order against his home, something that encapsulates the themes of the album, both an attachment to place and a resentment of unfeeling bureaucracy.

20th Century Man was released as a US-only single, in a much tighter edit (with two minutes lopped off the running time) but did not make the Hot 100.

Acute Schizophrenia Paranoia Blues

Writer: Ray Davies

Lead Vocalist: Ray Davies

And here we see Davies lightly (self-?)mocking the obsessions of the previous song's narrator. Over a honky-tonk background that sounds almost like the Lovin' Spoonful, with some lovely touches from the new horn section, Davies repeats the complaints of the previous song ("the income tax collector's got his beady eye on me" and "the man from the Social Security keeps invading my privacy") but here the previous song's passing mention of being "a paranoid schizoid product of the twentieth century" becomes the theme of the entire song. Along with the bureaucrats, the milkman, grocer and woman next door are all watching the narrator, who has been diagnosed with "acute schizophrenia disease".

While the song is done with a light touch, it's actually a rather scarily accurate portrayal of mental illness. I worked on a psychiatric ward for several years, and one patient, who fancied himself a songwriter, wrote songs which are very, *very* close to this, both in the expression of paranoia and the self-mocking acknowledgement that these are symptoms of illness rather than events in the real world.

Given Davies' own well-publicised mental problems, one wonders just how tongue-in-cheek this actually is...

Holiday

Writer: Ray Davies

Lead Vocalist: Ray Davies

One of the best things on the album, this seems to be written from the same point-of-view as the previous two songs. A superficially cheery song about a holiday, sung by Davies with a cigar in his mouth, this becomes darker when you realise the narrator has been "sent away" on his holiday, rather than having gone voluntarily. Given the protestations ("I don't need no sedatives to pull me round/I don't need no sleeping pills to help me sleep sound") and the narrator's claim that he "had to leave the city 'cause it nearly broke me down", maybe this "holiday" is to some kind of beach-side hospital.

The narrator tries to make the most of a holiday which sounds like most of my experiences of beach-side holidays ("lying on the beach with my back burned rare/And the salt gets in my blisters and the sand gets in my hair/And the sea's an open sewer...") but he's clearly distressed and lonely.

Musically, as well as in the device of the unreliable narrator, this seems to owe a lot to some of Randy Newman's music, with the simple chord sequence (most of the songs on this album are far more harmonically simplistic than those on earlier albums) played on piano with horn backing having a very New Orleans feel.

Skin And Bone

Writer: Ray Davies

Lead Vocalist: Ray Davies

A wonderful little song, this seems to have started as a parody of the Newbeats' *Bread and Butter*, which has a near-identical chord sequence (both songs have a I-V-I-V chorus in G, though *Skin And Bone*'s verse also has a IV chord and a passing IV# which aren't in the earlier track) and whose lyrics ("I like bread and butter/I like toast and jam... She don't cook mashed potato/She don't cook T-bone steak") are very close to those of this song ("She don't eat no mashed potatoes/She don't eat no buttered scones".) The similarity is most pronounced on the choruses, when there is a falsetto harmony, low in the mix, which sounds very like the Newbeats' vocalist. Davies has combined that song with a touch of the old spiritual *Dem Dry Bones* to create this song.

Lyrically, the song is an ode to what is now referred to as Health At Every Size, telling of a woman ("fat flabby Annie") who was "incredibly big and weighed about sixteen stone" before being put on a diet by "a fake dietician". The result? "She used to be so cuddly... but oh what a sin, now she's oh so thin" and she's "living on the edge of starvation", has "lost all the friends she had" and "looks like skin and bone" and "looks as if she's ready to die".

It may seem that this song has little to do with the wider political themes of the album, but in fact it fits them very well. The diet is portrayed as a new-fangled foreign import (Annie's also started to "do the meditation and yoga"), and the subtext is that one should remain true to oneself, not go trying to change, and especially not try to change to be more like a foreigner.

Alcohol

Writer: Ray Davies

Lead Vocalist: Ray Davies

Musically a beautiful mixture of hard rock and Kurt Weill, this song tells the story of an adulterous, drunken wife-beater and blaming every problem in his life on the women rather than on him. The Weillesque music manages to put this lyric in inverted commas, enough that it is clear that even though the song has a third-person narrator, he is still singing from the protagonist's point of view.

Davies' own relationship with the "demon alcohol" apparently informed this song. Davies is apparently a very light drinker, but alcohol affects him very badly thanks to the pain medication he takes for his bad back. Unsurprisingly, then, the alcohol in this song is more like a force of nature than something that people willingly consume.

Complicated Life

Writer: Ray Davies

Lead Vocalist: Ray Davies

Of all the songs on the album, this is the one that speaks to me the most. A simple three-chord country blues song with some nice slide guitar from Dave Davies (whose slide guitar tone is incredibly similar to his singing voice), this is one of the few songs on the album that look at the downside to the anti-modernist attitude Ray Davies takes for most of the record.

Our protagonist visits the doctor, complaining of "a pain in my neck, a pain my heart, and a pain in my chest", and is told he's ill from the stress caused by the complications of modern life, and that he needs to simplify his life considerably.

So far, so standard Ray Davies, but here the protagonist stops seeing women, drinking, going to work, exercising or doing anything else that causes him stress. And the result? He becomes unemployed and unemployable, has no food, has bills he can't pay, and is more stressed than he was to start with.

It's one of the few laugh-out-loud songs on the album, and one of even fewer to acknowledge that "the simple life" is not a panacea – and that makes the almost suicidal chorus of "life is overrated...got to get away from the complicated life" all the more easy to relate to. Yes, 20th (and 21st) century life is hard – but it's hard precisely because the alternatives are even harder so we're trapped in it.

In this song, by acknowledging that while he can see a problem he can't necessarily see the solution, Davies redeems the album – it's not just a political polemic for a return to an imagined golden age, but a work of art that's trying to engage with the complexities of the real world.

Here Come The People In Grey

Writer: Ray Davies

Lead Vocalist: Ray Davies

Musically, this is a chugging 12-bar blues in C, patterned after the work of bands like Canned Heat (the lead guitar part references their *Let's Work Together*), with little to distinguish it.

Lyrically, it's a story of one man's descent into madness, except that he's not going to be taken away by "the men in white coats", but by the more sinister, because duller, "people in grey".

Our protagonist's house is scheduled for demolition by the government (a recurring nightmare of the middle class Englishman in the mid-twentieth century – see the first episode of *The Hitch-Hiker's Guide To The Galaxy*, or the Mr Pilgrim referenced earlier.) And like all good liberals he doesn't want to fill in a load of forms that the government are forcing him to fill in in order to legitimise this destruction.

But his response is to go and live in a tent with his "baby", refuse to pay any rent or rates, and to take a gun with him to use against any policemen. Once again we see Davies' main theme in this album – that the impersonal forces of bureaucracy are putting so much pressure on anyone who wants to be an individual that they're likely to snap mentally.

Having not lived through this time period myself, I can't say if that was actually the way things seemed in the early 70s, but while this is nowadays the lament of the *Daily Mail* reader, it does seem to have been a common complaint right across the political spectrum in the 70s and 80s (see the aforementioned *Hitch-Hiker's Guide*, Terry Gilliam's marvellous film *Brazil*, the work of scriptwriter Robert Holmes, *Yes, Minister* and so on) the perception was of a world governed by unimaginative little men who would gladly cut bits off people in order to make them fit the box they were meant to fit into.

Have A Cuppa Tea

Writer: Ray Davies

Lead Vocalist: Ray Davies

One of the slightest songs on the album, this is very much a cousin of *Harry Rag*, this time singing the praises of tannin rather than nicotine. For most of the song it's a three chord singalong in praise of the healing properties of tea ("It's a cure for chronic insomnia/It's a cure for water on the knee"), but it once again quotes another song (a recurring motif in this album is the reuse of bits of old popular songs), *Sugartime* (a hit in the US for the McGuire Sisters, but Davies probably knew either Alma Cogan's UK hit version or Johnny Cash's cover version.) The "tea in the morning, tea in the evening" bit is a direct quote from the "sugar in the morning, sugar in the evening" refrain of the earlier song.

This is Davies trying to go back to the style he was using on *Something Else* and *Face To Face*, for the last time for many years, but it doesn't really work – at that time he was concentrating on sophistication in his music and lyrics, while this is an album that generally eschews artifice in favour of emotional honesty.

Holloway Jail

Writer: Ray Davies

Lead Vocalist: Ray Davies

A dark story song in the tradition of *Big Black Smoke*, this tells how the protagonist's girlfriend fell in with a "spiv" who framed her for a crime he'd committed. Musically, it's a rewrite of the old blues song *St James' Infirmary*, but with an incongruous line from the Everly Brothers' *Bye Bye Love* (written by Felice and Boudleaux Bryant) thrown in – compare the lines "She was a lady, when she went in" and "She was my baby, til he stepped in".

Oklahoma USA

Writer: Ray Davies

Lead Vocalist: Ray Davies

An absolutely lovely song, based around a repeating piano figure that almost acts as a drone, this ties together all the themes of the album in one beautiful, simple song – the monotony of British working-class life, and the dream of the America of films (and particularly in this case the America of film musicals) as the closest thing to a dream of heaven permitted in a society where even dreams are commercialised.

It's just a touching little song about a woman who dreams of being "in Oklahoma U.S.A./With Shirley Jones and Gordon McRea", but it's quite, quite beautiful. There's almost no harmonic movement in the main piano part (which for the most part plays simple arpeggios in A, D or E) but there's a lot more implied in the interplay of the various instruments and the vocal lines – just as there's more implied than said in the lyrics. The repeated line "All life we work but work is a bore,/If life's for living then what's living for?" in this context is absolutely heartbreaking.

On the next album, Davies would return to this theme in *Celluloid Heroes*, widely regarded as one of his best songs, but that song sounds like a less-good attempt at writing this, the emotional heart of this album.

Beautiful.

Uncle Son

Writer: Ray Davies

Lead Vocalist: Ray Davies

Another simple three-chord song, this one is about the Davies' brothers' uncle Son, who was apparently an active socialist, but one who felt let down by leaders of all sorts.

While this album is conservative, by the definition used in this very song – "Liberals dream of equal rights/Conservatives live in a world gone by/Socialists preach of a promised land" – it's a very strange, anti-authoritarian conservatism. Nowhere else I can think of would one get the reactionary overall feel of this album coupled with a chorus like "Bless you uncle Son/they won't forget you when the revolution comes".

With a verse like "Unionists tell you when to strike/Generals tell you when to fight/Preachers teach you wrong from right,/They'll feed you when you're born, and use you all your life", Davies seems, in sentiment if not in satiric skill, to be writing from much the same type of anger as Jonathan Swift – as Orwell described it in *Politics vs Literature*, "Politically, Swift was one of those people who are driven into a sort of perverse Toryism by the follies of the progressive party of the moment."

Davies seems to have a real anger against authority, to be almost physically pained by the destruction of working-class communities, and over and again in this album talk of revolution or armed insurrection comes up. Yet in the end (as we see especially in *Complicated Life*) he feels this is hopeless – the revolution is just another dead end, and all that is left is a retreat into the past, or into dreams.

Which is not a position I can agree with, but it's one with which I can definitely sympathise.

Muswell Hillbilly

Writer: Ray Davies

Lead Vocalist: Ray Davies

And we end with yet another three-chord song (actually six chords, but only because there's a key change up a tone after the first chorus), this time seeing the slum clearances (when people were moved out of rough, often dilapidated or war-damaged, poverty-stricken areas of inner cities into newer suburban or small-town areas which quickly became even worse to live in than the original slums) as an attempt "to build a computerised community", but our narrator vows "they'll never make a zombie out of me".

Meanwhile, the narrator's "heart lies in old West Virginia" – while he's never been to America, he sees the America of the cinema, and particularly the Wild West, as a symbol for the freedom that is being denied those who are being "put... in identical little boxes".

Bonus Tracks

Mountain Woman

Writer: Ray Davies

Lead Vocalist: Ray Davies

Another song with vaguely calypso rhythm, a la *Apeman*, but performed more in the style of Creedence Clearwater Revival, this isn't a particularly good song, but probably should have made it to the album proper anyway. That's because it paints America, the promised land of so many songs on the album, as being exactly like the Britain he described in the other songs – here a couple who live in the mountains have their home taken from them by the government so they can build a hydroelectric power station, and get moved to the thirty-first floor of an apartment block.

Kentucky Moon

Writer: Ray Davies

Lead Vocalist: Ray Davies

This song has more chords in it than almost the entire rest of the album, and shows that Davies was making a very deliberate choice to limit himself harmonically. While it's a sloppy performance, which sounds like a quick demo, the combination of Dave Davies' slide guitar against the ninth chords in the piano is very effective.

The lyrics are possibly slightly too literal – "Never been to Kalamazoo/Never been to Timbuktu...Making up tunes in hotel rooms/'bout places I've never been to" – and they make the themes of the album a little too explicit, but it's still a decent song.

If I've apparently given short shrift to many of these songs, it's because as individual songs they don't all stand up especially well – this is a much, much simpler set of songs than anything the band had done in years, and musically is much like the "back to our roots" sound that had dominated 1968-9 with albums like *John Wesley Harding* and the Beatles' *Get Back* project. As ever, the Kinks were just a little behind the times. There's a lot less to say about a three-chord blues song than there is about something as artfully constructed as, say, *Autumn Almanac*.

But that doesn't mean that Ray Davies had lost his talent – this is meant to be heard as an album, not as a set of individual songs, and the cumulative effect of the album makes it much better than the sum of its parts. Other than the *Something Else/Village Green/Arthur* trilogy, this may be the best album the Kinks ever made.

Everybody's In Showbiz

Everybody's In Showbiz is possibly the most overlooked album from the Kinks' early period. A rather odd double-album, the second disc is made up of live recordings, almost entirely of songs from the previous two albums (the CD reissue adds two 60s classics – *Til The End Of The Day* and *She's Bought A Hat Like Princess Marina* – but other than the three cover versions dealt with below, the original live recording contained one song from *Arthur*, two from *Lola vs Powerman* and five from *Muswell Hillbillies*), while the consensus about the first disc, of new studio recordings, is that it is mostly a rock star whinging about how terrible the life of a rock star is, with the occasional song that sounds like an outtake from *Muswell Hillbillies*.

But while this consensus is, in fact, accurate, it slightly misses the point. Putting out a live album that is almost entirely devoid of hits is in itself a fairly odd thing to do, but to couple a live album with an album of songs about how awful touring is – songs that if one has any empathy for the singer sap any semblance of joy from the live recordings that follow – has to be a deliberate artistic statement.

And while almost every rock musician of the 70s released an album about how awful life on the road was, the life of the Kinks at the time *was* truly awful. Dave Davies had recently had a breakdown – what sounds from his later descriptions like a psychotic episode lasting a few months – and communication between the two brothers was so bad at the time that thirty years later Ray Davies claimed not to be aware it had happened. Meanwhile, the band had by the time of this album been obsessively touring the USA for three years, trying to slowly rebuild the audience they'd lost there in 1965, and Ray and Rasa Davies' marriage was coming to an unhappy end, leading to another in Ray Davies' increasingly frequent bouts of mental illness.

What we get, as a result, is an album that is almost entirely about dissociation — about having no emotional connections to either one's environment or to the surrounding people. Sometimes this makes the songs come off as affectless and difficult to empathise with, but at other times there's a surprising beauty to the songs, although they remain in the simple style of *Muswell Hillbillies*, with little musical invention when compared to Davies' work from 1966 through 69.

(This review will primarily deal with the studio songs, only looking at the live cover versions that don't appear elsewhere.)

Studio

Here Comes Yet Another Day

Writer: Ray Davies

Lead Vocalist: Ray Davies

In what sounds almost like an overture to the album, like a curtain is rising, Ray Davies here sings about the grinding monotony of the touring life, with lyrics that have little rhythmic variation but come so fast that lines overlap, over a clomping rock beat and what amounts to a single chord (in the middle eight the guitar very briefly throws in a passing IV chord a couple of times, and goes to V before the change back to the verse, but otherwise the entire thing is all on a single I chord.)

It succeeds all too well in conveying the dullness and repetition of touring, as even at only 3:30 it seems a good minute and a half too long.

Maximum Consumption

Writer: Ray Davies

Lead Vocalist: Ray Davies

This is one of several songs on the album that seem obsessed with food. In this case, over a harmonically simple backing very much in the *Muswell Hillbillies* mode, Davies talks about food (specifically *American* food – clam chowder, beef steak on rye, pumpkin pie and so on are foods that Davies would only have been eating on tour in the US) as fuel, and himself as a machine that needs refuelling – "I'm a maximum consumption, non-stop machine /Total automation, perpetual motion."

Even the sexual innuendo here ("I'm so easy to drive, and I'm an excellent ride") is all about the body as machine.

In the context of the album as a whole, then, this is another song about detachment – the focus in this, as in several songs on the album, is on the functions of the body rather than the mind inside it. After becoming detached from his home country and the people around him, the protagonist of the song (who in this case, as with much of the album, we probably can identify with Davies in a way we can't always with earlier songs) is starting to think of his body, too, as something other, something separate that's moving around independently of his wishes, a machine that requires food and sex.

Unreal Reality

Writer: Ray Davies

Lead Vocalist: Ray Davies

Musically, this song is not one of Davies' best – he's continuing here (and on much of the rest of the album) his *Muswell Hillbillies* habit of writing with only standard rock & roll changes, and his ideas are wearing thin. This song is almost entirely made up of just I, IV and V chords (with one brief move to ii, on the line "Because they can touch it, it's gotta be reality") and sounds like it was written by a computer asked to generate a *Muswell Hillbillies*-esque song.

Lyrically, though, this is the most disturbing of all the songs on the album, and really the lyrical key to the entire thing. This could almost have been written by a Philip K Dick protagonist, and portrays someone getting more and more detached from reality. Normal Kinks targets (the businessman in his suit and tie who seems like he's made of plastic) merge with the strange environment of a foreign country, with its towering buildings that "reach... right up to the clouds", and convince our narrator that he's in an unreal world.

Here *Muswell Hillbillies'* longing for 'authenticity' has turned sour – our narrator is convinced that the 'inauthentic' experiences he's having are literally, not metaphorically, unreal. He's so detached from his surroundings that he worries they're hallucinations.

Hot Potatoes

Writer: Ray Davies

Lead Vocalist: Ray and Dave Davies

A five-chord song, the most harmonically complex thing we've had so far, though still rudimentary compared to the band's pre-RCA work (this time with a guitar line that seems to be parodying George Harrison's guitar on *My Sweet Lord* and a piano part that sounds like it was inspired by the Small Faces' *Lazy Sunday*), this is another one that makes the connection between appetite for food and sexual appetites, as the protagonist's wife won't "satisfy his appetites" with anything other than hot potatoes unless he goes out to work.

The lyrics are confused and don't make much literal sense, but again there's an emphasis on the carnal, on the needs of the body, as the relationship between the protagonist and his wife is deteriorating.

Sitting In My Hotel

Writer: Ray Davies

Lead Vocalist: Ray Davies

Easily the best song on the album, this is a piano-based ballad with a simple chord structure and a return of the fragmented descending basslines that Davies had used so effectively in earlier songs. The descending bassline clearly makes Davies think of baroque music, and so we have some lovely fanfare-like baroque trumpet playing from Mike Cotton over the top.

Musically the song sounds like an experiment in writing musical theatre (something the song comments on itself, with the line about "writing songs for old-time vaudeville revues"), and has a lot in common with the more singer-songwriter end of glam – it could easily fit on David Bowie's *Hunky Dory* album, for example.

Lyrically, once again this is about alienation – being away from one's friends and acting in a way that doesn't feel natural. The protagonist wonders what his friends back home would think if they could see him "Dressing up in my bow tie/Prancing round the room like some outrageous poof" (Davies has an unfortunate tendency to associate homosexuality, theatricality and artificiality, even as he is ambivalent about the first, fond of the second, and scathing about the last.)

The whole thing paints a touching picture of someone trying to hold on to his old values and use them to re-evaluate a life that seems to have gone horribly wrong.

Motorway

Writer: Ray Davies

Lead Vocalist: Ray Davies

A fun track, this is actually the second-best comedy country song of the 1970s about how bad motorway service station food is[19] – a subject close to the hearts (and stomachs) of many touring bands then and now. Based on one chord for the most part (expanding to four chords for the middle eight), this features some nice country guitar picking in a bluegrass style, while John Dalton's bass part is clearly influenced by Marshall Grant's simple tic-toc root/fifth parts on Johnny Cash's records.

Once again, though, this is a song about detachment from one's normal life, travelling and thinking only in terms of basic bodily functions – eating cold meat pies, using filthy toilets and sleeping in cheap hotels. Davies, here, is living a life in which every sense is being battered and he's being ground down, and once again he's trying to reach out to anyone from his home life – "Mama oh mama, my dear Suzi too, This motorway message is sent just for you".

You Don't Know My Name

Writer: Dave Davies

Lead Vocalist: Dave Davies

A welcome return of Dave Davies as a songwriter, after two albums on which he didn't have a single song, this is another

---

[19] The best, of course, being *Watford Gap* by Roy Harper

song about dissociation and travelling, done in a country-rock style that sounds spookily like Ronnie Lane's songs for the Faces (which featured Rod Stewart, an old schoolmate of the Davies brothers who had briefly sung in a band with them in the very early 60s), but with an incongruous jazz-folk flute part that makes this one of the most interestingly-arranged tracks on the album.

Supersonic Rocket Ship

Writer: Ray Davies

Lead Vocalist: Ray Davies

The Kinks' last UK hit single of the 1970s, this reached number 16. Musically, it's an attempt to rewrite *Apeman*, but actually has a far more convincing calypsonian feel to it than the earlier song did, with an arrangement that puts the country dobro sound Dave Davies has been using for much of the last two albums up against a convincingly Trinidadian-sounding horn section and steel drums.

Unfortunately, Ray Davies uses his comedy Carribean accent for most of the song, as it would be quite lovely otherwise. In this song about escaping from pressures, the "supersonic rocket ship" here plays much the same role that the train to heaven does in older spirituals. But unlike almost everything else on the album, here Davies is looking outward – he's offering to "take you on a little trip/my supersonic ship's at your disposal if you'd be so inclined", making an offer rather than trying to persuade, and to someone else rather than looking inward.

And it's a generous-spirited offer, too – an offer of a trip to a world where no-one shall be enslaved by poverty or conformity ("On my supersonic rocket ship, nobody has to be hip, nobody needs to be out of sight/Nobody's gonna travel second class, there'll be equality and no suppression of minorities".) Davies had always hated the pressure to conform to what was considered cool, as far back as *Dedicated Follower Of Fashion*, and here he explicitly places that kind of conformism on a par with the other kinds of conformism that the hip, then and now, were happier with him satirising.

There's probably a slight element of sexual double-entendre to the lyrics, but it's very slight, and for the most part this should be taken sincerely as being about a desire to escape – but in a more generous, openhearted way than many of Davies' more misanthropic songs.

So it's a shame that with the misjudged vocal he turned what could have been one of his best songs into a novelty number, but there's still substance here if you listen for it.

Look A Little On The Sunny Side

Writer: Ray Davies

Lead Vocalist: Ray Davies

Utterly different from anything else on the album, this is arranged primarily for the horn section and is vastly more harmonically complex than the rest of the record, with descending basslines, drone notes held at the top of the horn stack and so on leading to chords like a V♭aug going to iv with a VI♭ in the bass.

It's also practically the Kinks' only real excursion into a music-hall style. The term 'music hall' gets applied to the band all the time by lazy rock journalists, but in truth almost none of the band's songs have any real relationship to any of the many styles that were performed in the music halls – the songs that usually get labelled that way tend to have more in common with the songs written for comedy revues by people like Flanders & Swann than with the working-class music hall tradition.

This, on the other hand, could easily fit on a bill with actual music-hall songs like *I Do Like To Be Beside The Seaside* or

I Live In Trafalgar Square, at least musically. Lyrically, it's a different matter — while the title is definitely one that fits the style, the song is actually about not letting bad reviews of your music get you down.

This song is, lyrically, pretty much thoroughly defended against any kind of critique, because it argues that no matter what kind of songs you write, a critic will always say it's not as good as your older stuff or that you should work in a different style. Therefore, I won't say anything about the lyrics — anything I could say about them, good or bad, they've already pre-empted.

Celluloid Heroes

Writer: Ray Davies

Lead Vocalist: Ray Davies

And the studio part of the album finishes with this, one of the Kinks' most-loved songs. Unfortunately, I have to be a bit of a contrarian here, and say that I simply don't see what the fuss is about with this one. At six minutes and twenty-two seconds, it's at least three minutes too long for the limited musical ideas.

It's overblown and bombastic, and seems to my ears like an unsuccessful rewrite of *Oklahoma, USA* that Davies has for some reason tried to turn into *Hey Jude* instead. All the real emotion of the earlier song has been replaced with cloying sentiment, and it's very much of a piece with Elton John's *Candle In The Wind*, with its expressions of pity for the lives of film stars from the golden age of Hollywood.

Fundamentally, I can't see the appeal of this song, but this may well be a fault with me — to most Kinks fans this is the band's last true classic.

Live

Mr. Wonderful

Writer: Jerry Bock, George David Weiss and Larry Holofcener

Lead Vocalist: Ray Davies

A thirty-second live snippet of a song from a musical, made famous by Peggy Lee, with Davies putting on an exaggerated crooner voice.

Banana Boat Song

Writer: Irving Burgie and William Attaway

Lead Vocalist: Ray Davies

A brief one-minute run-through of part of the traditional calypso song.

Baby Face

Writer: Harry Akst and Benny Davis

Lead Vocalist: Ray Davies

A return to the Mike Cotton Sound's trad jazz roots, with a cover of the 1926 Al Jolson song, done in an approximation of the style of Louis Prima.

Preservation

Act One

Preservation Act One is an incredibly difficult album to write about. Hearing the Kinks' albums in sequence, it sounds like something of a return to form, a return to more complex structures and interesting melodies after a long run of rock albums based on simple three-chord songs. The band's musical palette expands again, with the Kinks and their horn section (now minus Mike Cotton) joined by a backing vocal chorus, and with many songs featuring strings and more complex keyboard parts.

But in fact it's the last gasp of that kind of songwriting from Ray Davies, and from this point on the Kinks are a rock band, as opposed to a pop one.

Partly, *Preservation Act One* gives a misleading impression because it was never intended to be heard in this form. Originally, *Preservation* was intended as a single piece – a narrative work based on, and expanding upon, the themes of *Village Green Preservation Society* as well as the material about the destruction of communities in *Muswell Hillbillies*, but the album took much longer to complete than originally intended, after Ray Davies scrapped the initial sessions, and so it was released in two sections.

Act One, as a result, just introduces us to the characters who will take part in the narrative (and to some who won't be heard of again), with the actual story relegated to the double album *Act Two*. Anyone who's ever heard a concept album will immediately see the problem here.

The recording of *Preservation Act One* was also the culmination of many of the problems in Ray Davies' life. In the middle of the recording, on Davies' twenty-ninth birthday, his wife Rasa left him, taking their two daughters with her, and for a while it looked as if the Kinks themselves were going to split up.

The band pulled through – and eventually both Davies brothers became much more stable – but as they moved first to concept albums and then to arena rock, *Preservation* , and especially *Preservation Act One*, is the last point at which the Kinks sound like their mid-60s peak.

Preservation (Non-Album single)

Writer: Ray Davies

Lead Vocalist: Ray Davies

This song is misplaced on the CD, and both song and album suffer for it. This track was actually a single, released several months after *Preservation Act Two*, which sums up the plot of the entire piece in one three-and-a-half-minute hard rock track.

For what it is, this is decent enough – it's a three-chord glam stomper that wouldn't have sounded at all out of place on 70s rock radio, with a catchy guitar riff – but the lyrics are just a giant infodump rather than being particularly clever or moving.

More importantly, though, the album itself is quite cleverly, and deliberately, structured, moving from the quiet of *Morning Song* to the loud rock of *Demolition*, and by starting the CD with a song in the style of the last track, that structure is ruined.

ACT ONE

Morning Song

Writer: Ray Davies

Lead Vocalist: Chorus

The *actual* album opener is this utterly gorgeous little piece, which sounds like it features none of the Kinks at all. Rather, it is a piece for strings, woodwind and wordless vocals, building up from a single violin and a humming bass vocal, singing something that is halfway between Paul Robeson's version of *Shenandoah* and the Largo from Dvorak's *New World Symphony* (the piece which this most resembles.) Slowly a choral backing is added, along with a second, female lead vocalist, who sings along with the violin in a manner similar to Vaughan Williams' *Sinfonia Antarctica*, creating an almost theremin-like effect, before ending with a massed choral chord.

It's utterly unlike anything else in the Kinks' catalogue, but a perfect opener to the album.

Daylight

Writer: Ray Davies

Lead Vocalist: Ray Davies (as Chorus)

The scene-setter for the album, this song starts with a simple three-chord acoustic guitar and organ based verse, with a constant D pedal note giving it a vaguely Indian feel, while the backing chorus singing the word "daylight" has almost a gospel air.

After twenty bars of this, the song changes key, up a fifth, for the next passage (the line "another night has gone away and here comes yet another day" is a transitional passage I'm choosing to include with the verse.) We're suddenly in a totally different musical world – the brass band style music here evoking park bandstands – as the melody keeps ascending, with two Ray Davieses overlapping with each other as they go up the scale (starting on the fourth of the scale, making what Davies is singing a Lydian mode scale.)

The second time through this scale it continues up past the high fourth and onto the seventh, which then becomes the fourth of B – another key change up a fifth. We repeat the scale twice more in the new key, before, on the line "feel that daylight", moving back to the original key of D via an implied change to E.

These changes up a fifth are both natural key changes for this kind of music – brass band music makes much use of fifths because they're easy to play on brass instruments – but the continuous rising feel of the song also evokes the sun rising and the sky getting brighter quite beautifully.

If you hadn't heard *Lola vs Powerman*, *Percy*, *Muswell Hillbillies* or *Everybody's In Showbiz*, this would be what you'd expect a new Kinks track to sound like.

Lyrically, it's less interesting, just painting a picture of the world we're going to explore over this album and the next, but taking the albums in order it sounds like the band reversing out of a dead end, after they'd pushed the simple rock style as far as it could go, and going back to their old style to find another way forward.

Sweet Lady Genevieve

Writer: Ray Davies

Lead Vocalist: Ray Davies (as The Tramp)

Both the most heartbreaking, and in many ways the cleverest, song on the album, this non-charting single was Ray Davies' attempt to reach out to his estranged wife Rasa, begging for forgiveness, and may be the last truly *great* Kinks song.

In some ways, it's a reversion back to the style of the last few albums — it's based around strummed guitar chords and huffed harmonica, and while there's a little tonal ambiguity (it's mostly in A, but hints at the key of E on occasion), the chords are all play-in-a-day simplicity and the arrangement is straightforward, with no interesting instrumental parts. The only really different thing about the song musically is its utter metrical irregularity — there's a regular tic-toc rhythm in the drums, but the melody line and chord changes seem almost to ignore the bar lines.

But what makes this song so great is that even though it's clearly one of Davies' most emotionally honest songs, it's a song written from the point of view of a dishonest man. It's a song that had to be sung in character, and Davies makes the character seem utterly in the wrong — not only is he a liar, a cheat, and an alcoholic, he undercuts his own promises to change.

He wants her back, he promises to "take away all your sadness [if you] put your trust in me", but both he and the listener know that he'll never change and she'll never come back. He even laughs a little at the very thought that she'll return.

To be so artistically honest as to sabotage any possibility of reconciliation in the very song written to attempt to rebuild a marriage is something very few people could do. As a portrait of a failed relationship, and of a character who's half-deluding himself but is honest enough to see through his own delusions, this is almost on a par with Frank Sinatra's *Watertown*. This song does not make Davies look good at all, but I can think of few braver artistic works.

There's A Change In The Weather

Writer: Ray Davies

Lead Vocalist: Ray Davies (as Working Class Man, Middle Class Man and Upper Class Man)

One of the stronger songs on the album, this manages to blend the harder rock sound the band had been producing on recent albums very effectively with the more orchestrated feel of the music on the rest of this album, giving the best of both.

The song starts with a funk riff on guitar, with a Hammond pad and soulful horns, as Davies takes on three characters — a worker, a middle-class southerner, and an upper-class idiot. As the music repeats the same simple changes (with a key change up a fourth for the third repeat, as the upper-class man introduces himself), these three introduce themselves in a manner reminiscent of the "I know my place" sketch from *The Frost Report,* and we're told "there's trouble brewing". Then dropping back down to the original key, we get one more time through the changes as the three sing in unison about how "there's a change in the weather/we've got to learn to stick together".

And then we get a total change of instrumentation, dropping down to tuba, trombone and piano for two bars of common-time bridging material before going into a brass-band section in $\frac{6}{8}$ (with a bar of $\frac{4}{4}$ thrown in on "it will brighten".) Moving up a fourth, the song changes completely, and becomes about a positive, rather than a negative, change, as Davies sings in a light, mannered voice over a female backing singer "la la"ing in a joyful manner.

But then after this extended section, we go back to the original musical material, but here all hope and all funkiness has left — instead we have a ponderous, thudding, heavy metal beat with squealing atonal horns as multiple Ray Davieses sing "See the holocaust risin' over the horizon/Gonna see a manifestation, total chaos, devastation" and similar portents of doom.

After this material repeats in C then back in G, we once again drop into the cheerful section, here sounding more like a music-hall performance than a brass band, thanks to the more prominent piano part. Davies here sounds even more mannered, and we fade on a hopeful note from the brass. And all this comes in at less than three minutes.

There's a change coming, but whether it's a good one or not, we'll have to wait for the next album to see, when the story really gets going.

Where Are They Now?

Writer: Ray Davies

Lead Vocalist: Ray Davies (as The Tramp)

One of two really weak songs on the album, unfortunately programmed back to back, this sounds like an outtake from *Everybody's In Showbiz*. A nostalgic track looking back on the past, it was presumably meant to evoke similar emotions to some of the songs from *Village Green Preservation Society*, but rather than looking back on some mythical golden age of the past, it's only looking back at the late 50s and early 60s, and has nothing to say about that time, just lists a bunch of people (Mary Quant, Christine Keeler, Keith Waterhouse) and fictional characters (Jimmy Porter) who were quite well-known at that time and slightly less-well known a decade later, and asks "where are they now?", over a plodding background that sounds like *Like A Rolling Stone* on barbituates.

Musically, there's some similarity to the "all the people of the town" section of *Johnny Thunder*. This may be to try to tie the song in with the next one thematically.

One Of The Survivors

Writer: Ray Davies

Lead Vocalist: Ray Davies (as Johnny Thunder)

The other bad song on the album, this revisits Johnny Thunder from *Village Green Preservation Society*, finding him now heavier and greying, but still listening to the music he listened to when he was young.

Much like the previous song, this is about nostalgia for the (then-)very recent past, and consists almost entirely of lists of things, in this case 50s rock songs and performers (with an emphasis on slick white doo-wop like Dion & The Belmonts and Danny & The Juniors.) It's the musical equivalent of TV programmes of the *I Love 1983* type. It wins over the previous track in that it has some energy, but then extends what amounts to a minute or so worth of mediocre musical material to four and a half minutes, losing all goodwill along the way.

Cricket

Writer: Ray Davies

Lead Vocalist: Ray Davies (as The Vicar)

Side two of the album opens with this absolutely delightful track. A more coherent musical cousin of *Look A Little On The Sunny Side,* this features possibly the most real character Davies ever created — the Vicar.

The lyrics are a parody of a particular kind of Church of England sermon, the muscular, sporty, patriotic equivalent of Alan Bennett's *Beyond The Fringe* sermon ("Life, you know, is rather like opening a tin of sardines. We are all of us looking for the key"), an extended metaphor about how the devil will "try to LBW and bowl a maiden over", and "He'll baffle you with googlies/with leg breaks and offspin", but "keep a straight bat at all times, let the Bible be your guide, and you'll get by".

It's an absolutely perfect bit of observational comedy — he gets the speech patterns of this kind of vicar down exactly — and made all the funnier by the fact that Davies is clearly exaggerating something he genuinely thinks himself (he's well-known as a lover of cricket, and one can imagine him at least half agreeing

ACT ONE   189

that it's God's game because "It has honour, it has character and it's British".) There's also the possibility that the Vicar knows rather less about cricket than he's pretending, especially since he thinks cricket has "rules" when it has "laws".

This is possibly the most laugh-out-loud-funny thing the band ever did, and it's musically enjoyable as well. After two dull lists, the album has returned to a level of quality not seen since *Arthur*.

Money And Corruption/I Am Your Man

Writer: Ray Davies

Lead Vocalist: Ray Davies (as Mr Black) and chorus

And here we start to see the overarching story of the *Preservation* project come together. This is a medley of two songs, which put together have a very disturbing message.

We start with a song in the style of a traditional English folk-song – a pentatonic melody, in waltz time, over a quickly-strummed guitar, as a chorus of ordinary people sing about how "money and corruption are ruining the land/wicked politicians betray the working man" and "we're tired of hearing promises we know they'll never keep".

On its own, this would be just a better-than average example of the anti-politics theme that runs through much of Davies' work at this time. Politicians, yeah? They're all liars, right? Yeah...

But then the chorus sings "Show us a man who'll be our saviour and will lead us..." and we get the introduction of Mr Black, one of the two rival political leaders who dominate the next album.

The second of these songs, *I Am Your Man* , is sung by Mr Black, and is set to the most powerful music on the entire album. A gorgeous, sweeping ballad, with the return of the ever-descending chromatic basslines Davies used so much in the late 60s, this is soft, gentle, reassuring music that makes you think "yes, everything's going to be all right".

And over the top, Mr. Black persuades you to endorse a totalitarian dictatorship.

At first glance, Black's programme doesn't sound so different from that of the Labour party of the time, recently returned to power — nationalisation of major industries, slum clearances, support of unions, redistribution of wealth — but the clue is in the chorus. "Workers of the nation unite."

Not the internationalism of Marx and Engels — "Workers of *all* nations unite", but nationalism. And then you notice other things. The mention of a "five year plan". The mention of a "Fatherland".

This is almost as scathing a self-critique as *Sweet Lady Genevieve*, in other words. Davies has looked at the anti-politics mood of his then-recent albums, and seen that when people think that way, when they are disenchanted by politicians on all sides, is precisely when nationalism and extremism can sneak in in the guise of utopianism.

A miniature masterpiece.

Here Comes Flash

Writer: Ray Davies

Lead Vocalist: Dave Davies (as Chorus, with Scared Housewives)

And the other villain of the piece is now introduced — Mr Flash, the glamorous, slimy, showbiz politician who is opposed to Black.

This is an absolutely wonderful uptempo pop-rock song which manages to combine within its two minutes and forty-one seconds more different styles than many bands manage in a career. Starting with a Who-style clang of guitars, it moves into Dick Dale territory — very fast, heavily reverbed, staccato surf guitar, playing a vaguely Arabic sounding melody.

Then the voices enter, and they're singing pseudo-operatic falsetto, with very fast, tumbling lyrics, and suddenly it's the previously-unconceived middle ground between Dick Dale and W.S. Gilbert, and to emphasise the end of every line we have the most cavernous drum sound I've ever heard.

And then the orchestra and female chorus come in and add a baroque element, before the song finishes in a flourish with a theatrical fanfare taken from the *William Tell* overture.

Combining hard rock, pop, surf music and opera in one ridiculously exciting song, this is everything Queen ever wanted to be.

Sitting In The Midday Sun

Writer: Ray Davies

Lead Vocalist: Ray Davies (as The Tramp)

One of the catchiest things on the album, this was one of the first things the band recorded for the project (and probably the first song they recorded in Konk, their own studio), and was recorded before the start of the personal turmoil in Ray Davies' life that caused the darker tone of much of the songwriting on this album.

It's enjoyable and pretty, and was quite rightly released as the first single from the album, as it's definitely the most commercial-sounding thing on the record, echoing back to a mid-sixties summer pop sound and at times almost sounding like the Beach Boys. But it's ultimately a lightweight track — it's musically simplistic, and the lyrics, a paean to laziness and unemployment, are slight — so it's unfortunately easy to see why it didn't chart.

And a personal peeve of mine, which I accept most people won't share — in the chorus, the rhyme of "midday sun" with "currant bun" gets on my nerves (because "currant bun" only works because it's rhyming slang for sun, so he's just saying "sun" twice in effect), and then rhyming "reason" with sun and bun *really* doesn't work.

Demolition

Writer: Ray Davies

Lead Vocalist: Ray Davies and Dave Davies (as chorus and Flash)

And the closing track is, unfortunately, one of the weaker songs on the album. Very much like the track *Preservation* itself, this seems to have been written as a deliberate attempt at aping the sound of the Who, but with extra female backing vocals.

Musically, it sounds like an outtake from *Tommy*, but the lyrics are about Davies' old bugbear of compulsory purchase, and urban areas being regenerated into "a row of identical boxes".

Unfortunately, much as I'm not a fan of property developers in general, the combination of bludgeoning, riffy, hard rock and town planning is not one that works very well, and Dave Davies' impassioned scream of "Whaaa! Specifically designed for modern-day living!" may well be the most bathetic moment in the band's catalogue up to this point.

Nonetheless, it sort-of works, mostly thanks to Dave Davies' guitar playing, and it works as a bridge between act one and the much...odder...act two.

Act Two

And so we finish our look at the Kinks from 1964 to 1974 with this, the double-album sequel to *Preservation Act One*. Whereas *Act One* was mostly made up of songs that worked completely apart from their context, and had a whole cast of interesting characters, *Act Two* is about its plot.

Preservation is, as a whole, Ray Davies' attempt at writing a political musical along the lines of Brecht and Weill's work. Unfortunately, though, while Bertolt Brecht based his work on rigorous theories about both politics and aesthetics, coming up with works whose form perfectly fits their content (precisely because Brecht was trying to destroy normal unities of form and content), Ray Davies is not a particularly deep or original thinker.

That's not to deny his worth as an artist, of course – anyone who has read these essays will know that I think Ray Davies one of the greatest and most important songwriters of his generation – but Davies' work works on a primarily emotional level, and doesn't really suit being welded to a drama about the clash of political ideas.

Which isn't to say there is nothing of worth here. There are at least half-a-dozen fine songs on this double album, and apparently when pared down to a ninety-minute stage show, the *Preservation* albums became a riveting theatrical experience. But triple concept albums with spoken narration were never a great idea, and this is not an exception to the rule.

The plot is simply not strong enough to hold an album together without any truly great songs. It's an expression of Davies' political views, which from the evidence of this are a mixture of libertarianism, Burkean conservatism and small-government liberalism, mixed with a heavy dose of anti-politics. The evil capitalist dictator, Mr Flash, who wants to destroy everything good and traditional to replace it with flashy, exciting, modern things that will make him more money so he can have a good time, is defeated by the evil socialist dictator Mr Black, a Puritan who wants to destroy everything good and traditional to replace it with efficient uniformity and conformity. It's essentially the *1066 And All That* version of the Civil War ("Romantic But Wrong" versus "Repulsive But Right") reworked more cynically, so both sides are equally corrupt.

Other than Flash and his "floozies" and Black and his "do-gooders", the only other character here is the Tramp, the authorial mouthpiece of the first album now turned almost omniscient narrator, though we also have various between-track "Announcement"s from a newsreader (played by the actor Christopher Timothy, whose father had been a BBC announcer in the 1950s.)

There is merit here, but very little to suggest that this is the same band that had created masterpieces like *Waterloo Sunset* or *Days* only a few years earlier. Many of the songs here are almost impossible to talk about as standalone songs – they exist to move the narrative forward rather than for any aesthetic merit they may have – so my treatment of them here will be necessarily brief.

Introduction To Solution

Writer: Ray Davies

Lead Vocalist: Ray Davies (as The Tramp)

A simple rock song, in the style of the Who, based around a descending/ascending three-chord pattern (E-D-C-D-E), with the only change being a brief diversion to B and F#m on the line "But me, I'm only standing here".

The lyrics set the scene for the album – Mr Flash and his cronies are living the high life, drinking champagne, while there's rioting in the streets and Mr Black is planning to overthrow them, and meanwhile the Tramp is watching it all and wishing things were different.

ACT TWO

When A Solution Comes

Writer: Ray Davies

Lead Vocalist: Ray Davies (as Mr Black)

A song that definitely sounds of its time, this has the cocaine-infused sheen that was common to pretty much all mainstream rock of the mid-70s. Here Mr Black, "in an attic, somewhere in suburbia", dreams of his future revolution – he's been sitting on the sidelines, watching the collapse of civilisation, knowing that sooner or later people will turn to a strong leader, and then he can introduce his "final solution".

Not an especially subtle song, but largely accurate, I think, as to the psychology of fascism.

Money Talks

Writer: Ray Davies

Lead Vocalist: Ray Davies (as Mr Flash)

The first song on the album to sound like it might have been written primarily as a song, rather than as a narrative device, this is a four-chord glam rock song, seemingly very loosely based on Joe Tex's classic soul single *Show Me*. With a soul-style female backing chorus alternately doubling or echoing Davies' voice, this sounds like nothing so much as Marc Bolan's later work. It's one of the catchiest things on the album.

Lyrically, it's just a description of Flash's 'philosophy' – that no-one is incorruptible and that anyone will do anything for enough money.

Shepherds Of The Nation

Writer: Ray Davies

Lead Vocalist: Ray Davies (as Mr Black)

This is possibly the most interesting song on the whole album, as Davies seems, at least in part, to be examining the ways in which his own thinking can be twisted toward evil. (For all that I've occasionally criticised the way that Davies' politics seem simplistic, that doesn't mean that he's unaware of his own limitations, and the self-examination in his work is often painfully honest.)

A parodic rewrite of *The Village Green Preservation Society*, arranged in a pseudo-medieval style (with horns sounding almost like crumhorns and with vocals somewhere between madrigals and Gregorian chant), this is the dark side of "preserving the old ways from being abused/protecting the new ways for me and for you".

Fascism always looks to a golden age in the past (this is the main difference between fascism and totalitarian Communism – Communism looks to a golden age in the future instead), as much of Davies' work does, and usually combines that with some level of sexual puritanism, using that repression to motivate people to follow the great leader. And so here Mr Black uses rhetoric that isn't at all far from that used by people like the Festival Of Light or the National Viewers And Listeners Association – groups of religious fundamentalists that were becoming briefly popular in the mid-70s, as a reaction to the perceived excesses of the 'sexual revolution' and feminism, and who were essentially calling for an end to post-Enlightenment civilisation.

Black here lumps together supposed social evils like drugs and pornography with the basic human emotions that cause those things to be popular, so he calls for an end not only to pot and heroin, but to lust and lechery, to homosexuality, even to the existence of pubic hair.

And this is all wrapped up in the standard authoritarian demands for tougher punishment – the return of capital punishment, public flogging and the stocks.

Davies' politics, as expressed in his music, may be confused, and he may be all too keen to eulogise a past golden age, but when it comes down to a straight choice between homosexuals, dope smokers and pornographers on one side and authoritarians who want those people flogged and executed on the other, he knows which side he's on, and it's not the authoritarian one.

Scum Of The Earth

Writer: Ray Davies

Lead Vocalist: Ray Davies as Mr Flash

This is the cleverest song on the album, as well as possibly the best. Much of *Preservation*, as previously mentioned, is influenced by Brecht & Weill's *The Threepenny Opera*, and this song more so than anything else on the album.

Much as the previous song was a rewrite and critique of Davies' own *The Village Green Preservation Society*, this is a rewrite and critique of *What Keeps Mankind Alive?*, the best song by far from *The Threepenny Opera*. *What Keeps Mankind Alive?* is the most political song in the opera, and is an attack on capitalist moralisers, who keep the poor in poverty and then feign horror when they behave in an uncouth manner.

In the *Preservation* worldview, however, moralising (and 'do-gooding' generally) is the sin, not of capitalists, but of socialists. In Davies' eyes, a capitalist will destroy everything of value in the world for his own short-term benefit, while a socialist will destroy it all and claim it's for *your* benefit.

And so here, to a melody that is extremely reminiscent of *What Keeps Mankind Alive?* , Mr Flash defends himself against the attacks on him from Mr Black, using the same kind of argument that Macheath in the Threepenny Opera used to defend himself. He can't help being the way he is – society made him that way, and is it *his* fault society made him an unscrupulous exploiter? "if they could see deep inside me/They'd see a heart that once was pure/Before it touched the evils of the world". He quotes Shylock – "For if I cut myself I bleed, and if I catch a cold I sneeze/Have I not eyes to help me see? Have I not lungs to help me breathe" – in an attempt to emphasise the common humanity of the exploiter and the exploited.

It's a fairly decent point in some ways – if society is to blame for the faults of the poor, then surely it's equally to blame for the faults of the rich? – but of course it's an utterly self-serving one. The rich, unlike the poor, are in a position to do something to change things. Flash's crime isn't being "only human", but being selfish and amoral.

Second-Hand Car Spiv

Writer: Ray Davies

Lead Vocalist: Ray Davies (as Spiv)

This is a hard song to criticise, because while it's not much of a song as a *song*, as a piece of characterisation it's rather good.

Here Davies takes on the persona of a proto-Thatcherite 'entrepreneur', who started out on the dole (complete with standard Davies jab at the Welfare State, though here put into the voice of an unsympathetic character), and then worked his way up through being a secondhand car dealer to eventually becoming the owner of a multinational company and one of the most important people in the country.

The characterisation is perfect, right down to the accent – Davies sounds at times quite scarily like Lord Sugar – and is rather ahead of its time. This kind of figure would become a stereotype in the 1980s (think Loadsamoney or Del Trotter), but didn't really feature much in popular culture at the time. For all the banality of the story Davies is attempting to tell, his characters are all real types.

Musically, though, this is nothing interesting — the rock equivalent of those lesser Gilbert & Sullivan pieces where Sullivan just rum-tums through on autopilot because Gilbert has a lot of exposition to dump, except that Davies doesn't have anything like Gilbert's facility with language. Fast keyboard runs up and down the scale, and a brief musical quote from *Here Comes Flash*, aren't enough to bring this one to life.

He's Evil

Writer: Ray Davies

Lead Vocalist: Ray Davies (as Mr Black)

One of the catchier songs on the album, this is supposedly a party political broadcast by Mr Black, attacking Mr Flash, but it seems more to be just a warning to a specific woman that Flash uses women, drags them down to his level, and throws them aside. (Yes, it's supposed also to be a metaphor for how he's treating the country, but it's rather too literal for the metaphorical aspect to work particularly well.)

Musically, this is sort of proto-disco, with Mick Avory providing a straight four-on-the-floor bass drum and crotchets on the hi-hat in the intro (before settling down into a more conventional rock part, for much of the song, only returning to the disco feel for the instrumental break), and the track sounds at first like nothing so much as ABBA's *Money, Money, Money*, while later sounding more like ELO or one of the other bands who straddled the pop/prog/disco divide.

The verses are, like much of the material in *Preservation*, just Davies reciting lyrics over a simple backing track (to the same rhythm as the similar verses of *Demolition* and *Preservation*), but the choruses (where a cycle of fifths gets diverted by a brief change to the relative minor, so the changes go I-V-II-iv-VI rather than the expected I-V-II-VI) and the bridge (with a nice little Davies descending-semitones bassline is counterpointed by a rising female backing vocal) show a level of attention to the music that is absent from many of the songs on the album.

Mirror Of Love

Writer: Ray Davies

Lead Vocalist: Ray Davies (as Belle, Flash's Special Floosie)

The first single from the album, this is actually on the CD in two versions — the single version and the album version, which differ in a few points of arrangement and vocal performance, but are very similar.

Here Davies takes on the persona of Belle, Mr Flash's 'special floosie', an abused woman who can see that her boyfriend is unsuitable but sticks by him anyway. While it fits with the previous song, neither of them seem to have much of anything to do with the story, and one is again left with the impression that this would have been a much more coherent album had Davies got rid of the concept altogether and just released a single album of good songs rather than try to tie them to a flimsy narrative.

Musically, the song is a rather good effort at trad jazz — not at Dixieland, but specifically at trad, the British 1950s revival of the style, which had as much influence from jug band music and skiffle as from jazz. As a result it could almost be the work of a British equivalent of the Lovin' Spoonful or the Nitty Gritty Dirt Band, while still retaining some of the between-the-wars feel of some of the better material on the album.

The song is mostly driven by the horn section, who had built their career on this kind of material, and so carry it off with panache. It alternates between two sections — a simple major-key three-chord chorus in D (with lyrics about how Flash is OK seen "through the mirror of love"), and a slinky, more

ACT TWO

ambiguous verse. The verse lyrics alternate almost line-for-line between complaints and praise ("You're a crude and a rude lover/But I would have no other"), and the musical material is similarly ambiguous, starting out in Bm (the relative minor of the chorus' home key, a depressing key to be in) but slowly drifting into the key of A major (the fifth of the chorus' home key, a very happy key to go to.)

It's a simple but effective song, and Davies' vocals are probably his best on the album, with some wonderful jumps into a trilling falsetto a la Rudy Valee. The result is easily the best track on the album.

Nobody Gives

Writer: Ray Davies

Lead Vocalist: Ray Davies (as the Tramp)

And this song, more than any other, shows why I characterise Ray Davies' political views, as expressed through his songs, as being overly simplistic.

I can largely agree with his assessment that both untrammelled greed-driven capitalism and the kind of socialism that sees government control as an end in itself are evils – Mr Black and Mr Flash both do represent real types, the degenerate cases of two political philosophies that can, in the extreme, be harmful.

But the problem is, Davies doesn't seem to have gone any further in his thinking than an anti-politics shrug of "Well, they're all as bad as each other". And that leads to absurdities like this.

Because in this song, Davies (in character as the Tramp, who usually expressed Davies' opinions) complains that human nature is such that people fight over problems and take sides, rather than sitting down and talking problems over. He illustrates this with two examples of extremism, one from the left and one from the right.

The left-wing example he chooses is the General Strike of 1926, a strike that had more than a million people taking part, caused by attempts to cut the wages of miners, and which many people feared would lead to an actual revolution.

The right-wing example is the Nazi party, the Holocaust and the Second World War.

This is such a muddled piece of thinking that one doesn't really know where to start. The only thing the General Strike had in common with the Nazi dictatorship was that Winston Churchill was firmly opposed to both. One was a nine-day period of, admittedly quite extreme, industrial action attempting to prevent a drop in miners' wages, the other was twelve years of the worst horrors in human history, leading to the violent deaths of tens of millions of people. That's not the kind of comparison where "you're all as bad as each other" is really appropriate.

And this is the problem with having moderation as a principle. Sometimes one will end up taking a moderate position between two extremes because it happens to be the right position, but often one side clearly *is* worse than the other, and in those situations "you're all as bad as each other" is effectively the same thing as siding with the worse of the two sides.

One can quite easily set up left/right dichotomies where both sides are roughly equivalent. Had Davies compared Hitler with Stalin, he would have had a point. Likewise, had he compared the General Strike with, say, the three-day week that the Conservative government had introduced a few months before this album came out, he would have seemed relatively fair.

But faced with such a massively uneven balance, the song becomes absurd. Yes, the General Strike would possibly have been avoidable had all interested parties been willing to negotiate more. That's a fair criticism. On the other hand, one can't really imagine all the interested parties sitting down to negotiate a compromise between Hitler's aims and those of his enemies. The false equivalence here is so jarring that this one song pretty much single-handedly destroys any claim this album might have to be the serious work of political art that Davies intended.

Musically, the song is of little interest, being ridiculously overlong at 6:33, and bombastic with it.

Oh Where Oh Where Is Love?

Writer: Ray Davies

Lead Vocalist: Ray Davies (as The Tramp) and Marianne Price (as the do-gooders)

A pretty little tune, alternating between a $\frac{6}{8}$ folk style (sounding much like the kind of thing the Pogues would do a few years later) and a waltz-time section (the pulse only shifts slightly — one could easily transcribe both in $\frac{6}{8}$, but it seems stylistically to be better understood as a waltz) in a vaguely European style that once again conjures up thoughts of Weill. We also see the return of the Davies descending bassline, adding some harmonic interest to an otherwise fairly conventional structure.

Here for the first time we have a duet with Marianne Price, who takes lead vocals on several other songs on the album. Her voice is an intriguing one, having an untrained sound that is reminiscent of Rasa Davies', but singing in a lower range. Her slightly off-pitch, amateurish quality sounds a lot like Mo Tucker of the Velvet Underground, or the similar singing styles used by many waifish indie vocalists in more recent years, but is very different from the popular styles of the time. It's a gentle, sensitive performance, and the technical imperfections only add to that.

Lyrically, the song is the complaint of every reactionary, that things ain't what they used to be, and that people used to be nice and friendly and love each other and read fairytales, but now they're all rapists and murderers. But it's so clearly intended from the heart, and performed so well, that the track works anyway.

Flash's Dream (The Final Elbow)

Writer: Ray Davies

Lead Vocalist: none

Not really a song at all, but a four minute spoken dialogue between Mr Flash (played by Ray Davies in a bizarre, lisping accent that veers randomly between Cockney, comedy Jewish, Australian, South African, and what sounds like a prescient parody of the speaking voice of the singer Rufus Wainwright, often on a syllable-by-syllable basis) and his conscience, occasionally backed with snippets of *There's A Change In The Weather*, then going into a montage of vocal parts from songs from the first album, backed with a drum beat, and ending with a fanfare.

Utterly pointless.

Flash's Confession

Writer: Ray Davies

Lead Vocalist: Ray Davies (as Mr Flash)

Melodically, this is a variation on *Here Comes Flash*, with some slight musical differences, but re-harmonised to fit a chord sequence very similar to that of *Introduction To Solution*. Davies has clearly tried to repeat motifs throughout the album, but the motifs he's reused (the fast patter lyrics in rhyming couplets over four-chord vamps, for example) have tended not to be among the more interesting ones and have sounded more like a lack of ideas than an attempt at thematic unity – here,

ACT TWO

though, we can tell that this song is a summing up and closure of Flash's story, as he confesses his sins as he knows he's about to die.

This is one of the more startlingly modern sounding tracks on the album, as it sounds scarily like Bowie's Berlin period and some of the post-punk and new romantic bands influenced by those records.

As a song, it's not very good at all — it's another track that exists to fill in a gap in the story, rather than to be an enjoyable piece of music — but the production is interesting enough that it is not in the very lowest level of songs on the album.

Nothing Lasts Forever

Writer: Ray Davies

Lead Vocalist: Ray Davies (as Mr Flash) and Marianne Price (as Belle)

An absolutely lovely song, which was almost certainly inspired by Davies' marriage breakup. If in *Sweet Lady Genevieve* he still had some hope that his wife would return to him, here he knows that's not going to happen. In a heartbreaking duet, a resigned Mr Flash accepts that his relationship with Belle must end, but while she says it's for the best, he thinks otherwise.

It's impossible not to read lines like "I know that you'll survive/ And you'll get by/ Whatever/Though you say goodbye/ My love will never die/ It will last forever" as a message to his ex-wife, and it says a lot that Belle is here portrayed as a fundamentally decent person, who isn't happy about what she sees as the relationship's necessary breakup.

Both Davies and Price here sing at the very top of their ranges, straining for the notes, and this adds a real sense of emotion to the song — they've tried to make the relationship work, and can't, and the strain is showing.

While not one of the absolute top level of Kinks songs, this is one of the more touching of the post-*Arthur* songs, and very moving.

Artificial Man

Writer: Ray Davies

Lead Vocalist: Ray Davies (as Mr Flash and Mr Black) and Dave Davies (as Mr Black)

The second-longest actual song on the album is this attack on modernism – not modernity, it's an attack on the aesthetic of modernism, and in particular the way that many modernist political and aesthetic movements fetishise technology as an ends rather than a means. While the conflict between Flash and Black is framed as capitalism versus socialism, a more accurate way of looking at it would be to call it a clash between Modernism and Romanticism.

Here the Modernism has got as far as transhumanism – the master race Black is building would be one very recognisable to the inhabitants of websites like LessWrong. Black's creating an explicitly atheistic utopia full of technologically-augmented immortals, free of disease and pain. But these people are closer to the Cybermen from *Doctor Who* than any new, transcendent race – they've been created this way so Black can "Put your senses and your mind/ under constant observation/ even when you're dreaming". This is technology as a tool of oppression, rather than salvation.

Musically, the song comes in three sections. First we have a glam ballad, not dissimilar to Bowie's *All The Young Dudes* – presumably a deliberate resemblance, as Bowie had spent much of the previous few years singing about becoming *homo superior* in a manner which often outright endorsed fascism. The chord sequence for this section, obviously worked out on piano, is complex but based around the old Davies trick of keeping as many notes in the chord as possible the same while moving the bassline down a semitone at a time.

For the first time in the *Preservation* project we also get a welcome vocal contribution from Dave Davies, here sharing the Mr Black vocals with his brother.

We then have a second, faster section, sounding much like some of Elton John's faster songs, being driven in a similar way with fast, staccato piano chords – though the syrupy, over-orchestrated strings from the first section continue, and we have the addition of girl-group backing vocals singing "artificial, artificial man" over and over. This simple three-chord section then goes into an uptempo version of the first section, which leads to a key change from C to F.

We then have another two-chord section ("tell the world that we finally did it"), this time just playing ii-I in the new key, backed by acoustic guitar and drums, before repeating the second section, repeating the opening, slower section, and fading out on the "artificial man" vamp.

It's a complex structure, but it doesn't hang together wonderfully, and it's another song where one gets the impression that it was conceived for its narrative function rather than as a song that would work out of context.

Scrapheap City

Writer: Ray Davies

Lead Vocalist: Marianne Price (as Belle)

And once again we get a much shorter, tighter, better-conceived song covering some of the same ground straight after a flabby exposition-song. Here Belle describes the results of Black's revolution, with identical people living in "identical concrete monstrosities" and working identical jobs, with wildlife being destroyed because it's not efficient, and with manners and basic human decency a thing of the past.

This is a simple three-chord country song, based around the *Tumbling Tumbleweeds* bassline that Davies had used for *Holiday*, and with more than a little melodic resemblance to *Detroit City*, played by the core Kinks without the orchestration that had been augmenting them for much of the album.

You could play this to a thousand people without any of them guessing it was the Kinks, and it's not up to the standards of previous albums, but it's a pleasant track, and since in the twenty-nine minutes since *Mirror Of Love* we've had seven minutes of good songs and twenty-two minutes of exposition and bombast, it is a welcome relief as we draw near to the end of the album.

Salvation Road

Writer: Ray Davies

Lead Vocalist: Ray Davies (as 'everyone')

And the final song on the album is the anthem of Black's revolutionary movement (whose flute theme has been used in various forms to introduce the spoken announcements throughout the album.)

It's a curiously optimistic ending to the album, trying to find something positive in a new world, even after saying "goodbye freedom, hello fear", there's an acceptance that if the world is getting worse the only thing to do is not to look back at the better past, but try to make something good out of the future. It's a simple, catchy tune based on a play-in-a-day chord sequence, and follows a straight verse/chorus/verse/chorus pattern.

There's a subtlety to this song that's missing from much of the album, and the idea of having a triumphant sing-along anthem about how you might as well make the best out of a bad situation is vintage Davies.

And so we end the project that Ray Davies considers his most important work. Neither *Preservation* album is anywhere near as bad as its reputation suggests, but nor are they anything like good enough to carry the weight Davies intended. Apparently the tight, ninety-minute stage version the augmented band performed that year was much better, but unfortunately no film of those shows exist.

But there's worthwhile material in there if you dig, and in these days of iTunes, Spotify and so on, when people create their own playlists, it's possible to combine the best bits of both albums into something that stands up with their very best work[20]. Perhaps it's time for the better material on these albums to be re-evaluated.

Bonus Tracks

Slum Kids

Writer: Ray Davies

Lead Vocalist: Ray Davies and Dave Davies

This is a live recording from 1979, with a different line-up of the band (featuring Ian Gibbons on keyboards, and Jim Rodford, the former bass player of Argent who'd got his start playing with the Mike Cotton Sound in the 60s, on bass) performing a song which was written for *Preservation*, and which appeared in the stage show, but didn't make the album.

On this evidence, that's probably a good thing. This is a sub-Jimmy Rogers blues shuffle, with incredibly repetitive lyrics, repeating over and over that slum kids "never stood a

---

[20]For those with Spotify, my own attempt at doing this can be found at http://open.spotify.com/user/stealthmunchkin/playlist/0G58jzUnBPQfrigP0ztJuc

chance/We were dragged up from the gutter/On the wrong side of the tracks".

Possibly a hypothetical studio version would have been tolerable, but this version drags out what amounts to forty seconds of musical and lyrical material to six and a half minutes, partly through noodled solos but mostly through bludgeoning repetition. Not one of the band's finest moments.

Appendix: Non-Album Songs

A small number of songs were recorded by the Kinks over the years and released on compilations, but not included as bonus tracks on any of the CDs. In particular, two songs, *Til Death Us Do Part* and *Pictures In The Sand* were only ever released on the quickly-deleted early-70s compilation *The Great Lost Kinks Album*, while *When I Turn Off The Living Room Lights* is now available on the *BBC Sessions* set. These are dealt with below for completeness' sake.

Til Death Us Do Part

Writer: Ray Davies

Lead Vocalist: Ray Davies

This lovely little song, which is currently not in print, but is widely bootlegged, was recorded in 1968, one of the last things Pete Quaife worked on.

It was written for the film spin-off of the popular TV series *Til Death Us Do Part* (for American readers, the show was remade in the USA as *All In The Family*), but has little to do with the actual content of the film or TV show, being instead a banjo- and trombone-based piece of wistful nostalgia, from the point of view of someone who knows he's too old to change, and that the world is leaving him behind. Rasa Davies provides some lovely backing vocals.

It's a minor piece, but could easily have fit on *Village Green Preservation Society* or *Arthur,* and wouldn't have seemed out of place. Pye wanted to release this as a solo Ray Davies single, but Davies was uninterested.

Pictures In The Sand

Writer: Ray Davies

Lead Vocalist: Ray Davies

This outtake from the *Village Green Preservation Society* sessions is less interesting. Falling somewhere between Cockney knees-up and acoustic blues, and actually sounding very like the Small Faces' contemporary work, this is a curiously aimless track, and seems like an attempt at something that didn't quite come off. It would have made a fine B-side, because at this point even Davies' failures were enjoyable, but it doesn't seem like Davies was clear what he was doing here. It doesn't help as well that he's singing it in one of his 'funny' voices.

When I Turn Off The Living Room Light

Writer: Ray Davies

Lead Vocalist: Ray Davies

An absolutely hilarious little song, this was written for *Where Was Spring,* and falls into a long tradition of poems and songs written to a love who is less than conventionally attractive, such as Shakespeare's Sonnet 130. The narrator here tells his love that she "won't seem as ugly as you really are, when I turn off the living room light", before in the final verse admitting that "*we* won't feel as ugly as *we* really are, when I turn off the living room light".

The song has caused some controversy because of its opening line – "Who cares if you're Jewish, and your breath smells of garlic..." – which is fairly hard to defend. But this is one case where Davies really does seem to be writing from the point of view of a character, rather than himself (something his defenders have claimed with rather less justification about some of his more unpleasant late-70s work.) It's certainly not without its problems, but on balance I'd say it's funny, generous of spirit, and for all its faults well worth listening to.

Just like the Kinks themselves.

Acknowledgements

No book like this can be written without reliance on many other works. As well as the liner notes to the most recent and comprehensive set of CD reissues, the most frequently-consulted books during the writing of this volume have been *X-Ray* by Ray Davies, *Kink* by Dave Davies, *33 $\frac{1}{3}$: The Kinks Are The Village Green Preservation Society* by Andy Miller, *You Really Got Me* by Nick Hasted and *All Day And All Of The Night* by Doug Hinman. All of these come highly recommended.

The website kindakinks.net has also been an invaluable resource, and this book could not have been written without it.

Tilt Araiza, Jon Martin, Paul Ankers and Geoff Howe read through this book in draft form, and made many valuable suggestions.

All mistakes in the book, however, remain my responsibility, not theirs.

Special thanks go to Rachel Zall for her comments on *Lola*.

I would also like to thank my comic-blogging colleagues The Mindless Ones (http://mindlessones.com), Bill Ritchie, Steve Hickey, Lawrence Burton, Simon Bucher-Jones, Andrew Ducker, Andrew Rilstone, Gavin Burrows, Gavin Robinson, Alex Wilcock, Richard Flowers, Wesley Osam, Nicholas Whyte, Debi Linton, Jennie Rigg, Mat Bowles, Dave Page, Sarah Versau, Susan Lang and my parents, for their support during the writing of this book.

This book was written and typeset in the Free Software text editing program LyX (http://lyx.org), so thanks go to the creators of that software, as well as to the creators of LaTeX, and, ultimately, Donald Knuth, whose typesetting language TeX is the ultimate basis of all those programs. It was created on a machine running the Debian GNU/Linux distribution, so thanks to all the many thousands of people who gave their work freely to that system.

And I'd especially like to thank my wonderful wife, Holly Matthies, without whom neither this book or myself would exist in their present forms.

And finally, I'd like to ask you a favour. The careers of independent writers can be made or broken by their reviews on the websites from which their books are purchased. If you enjoyed this, please take a minute to go to the website you bought it from and post a review. On the other hand, if you find a problem with this book, please feel free to contact me by emailing andrew@thenationalpep.co.uk .